Dear Friends,

It's already dinnertime and everyone's home and hungry! Thank goodness for slow cookers because you're welcomed with a delicious aroma wafting from the kitchen. Instead of last-minute scrambling through the refrigerator or piling into the car for takeout food, your tossing a few ingredients into the slow cooker in the morning paid off! Just mix together a salad, cut up some bread and spoon out plates of steamy homemade stew. Then sit down with your family and catch up with the happenings of the day over a delicious meal.

Sounds too good to be true? ***Betty Crocker More Slow Cooker Recipes*** was created to help you make easy, delicious dinners, just like this—more than 130 of them. In just a few minutes in the morning or at your convenience, you can toss some ingredients in the slow cooker, turn it on and walk away.

You'll discover new favorites, from hearty main-course soups and zesty chilis to fork-tender roasts and stews chockfull of vegetables, herbs and savory spices. There are even special tip pages filled with great ideas to Celebrate Summer and make casual get-togethers a breeze with Potluck Pointers. And on those nights when there's really no time to cook, you'll reap the rewards of planning ahead when you whip up Great Ideas with Leftovers (and no one but you will know!).

With ***Betty Crocker More Slow Cooker Recipes,*** it's easy to have homemade on *your* schedule. Savor the possibilities!

Warmly,

Betty Crocker

Contents

Slow Cooking Made Simple, 6

1: Dips, Spreads & More, 11

2: Soups, Stews & Chilies, 37

3: Easiest-Ever Main Meals, 67

4: Meaty Main Dishes, 93

5: Beans & Veggies, 131

6: Make It & Take It, 159

7: Hassle-Free Holidays, 187

Helpful Nutrition and
   Cooking Information, 212

Metric Conversion Guide, 214

Index, 215

Slow Cooking Made Simple

In these days of drive-through dinners, fast food and canned convenience, the idea of slow cooking appears to be out of touch with the times. In reality, that couldn't be further from the truth. Slow cookers can save you time, money and energy. They allow you to "fix it and forget it," so you can spend precious time with family and friends, instead of in the kitchen. And if the simplicity of slow cooking doesn't convince you of its merits, the inviting aromas it sends throughout your house quickly will. Check out these slow-cooker secrets to help you make your recipes their slow-simmered best.

Secrets to Slow-Cooked Success

Like any other kitchen appliance, slow cookers come with a variety of options and features. Before you begin using your cooker, it's best to become familiar with how your model works.

As the name implies, continuous slow cookers cook food continuously by using a very low wattage. The heating coils, located in the outer metal shell of the cooker, remain on constantly to heat the crockery liner. Continuous slow cookers have two or three fixed settings: low (about 200°), high (about 300°) and in some models, auto, which shifts from high to low automatically. Some models feature removable ceramic liners. All recipes in this book were tested using continuous slow cookers. If you have an intermittent cooker (see box right), you'll need to follow the manufacturer's instructions.

Slow cookers come in a variety of sizes. One-quart cookers work well for dips and spreads, and 6-quart

Intermittent Cookers

Intermittent cookers have a heating element in the base and a separate cooking container that is placed on the base. The heat cycles on and off to maintain a constant temperature. Also, some intermittent cookers have a dial with numbers or temperatures rather than low, medium and high. The recipes in this cookbook have not been tested in an intermittent cooker. If you have an intermittent cooker, please follow the manufacturer's instructions for layering ingredients and selecting a temperature.

cookers are ideal for large cuts of meats and crowd-size recipes. For best results, make sure to use the slow cooker size recommended in the recipe. Slow cookers tend to work most efficiently when between two-thirds and three-fourths full of food.

Slow Cooker Tips and Tricks

These suggestions will help ensure all your slow-cooker meals are successful:

- Spray the inside of your slow cooker with cooking spray to make cleanup easier.

- Food in the bottom of the slow cooker will often be moister (from being in the cooking liquid), and meat, such as ribs, roasts and chicken, will fall off the bones sooner. Rotate meats halfway through cooking to help them cook evenly.

- Root vegetables, such as potatoes and carrots, take longer to cook, so cut them into smaller pieces and place them closest to the heat source, at the bottom of the cooker.

- Remove skin from poultry and trim excess fat from meats before cooking to keep fat and calories to a minimum.

- Cook and drain ground meats before adding them to the slow cooker.

- Brown meats and poultry in a skillet before placing them in the slow cooker. Although this isn't necessary, browning can enhance the finished flavor and appearance of your dish.

- Use dried leaf herbs instead of ground because they retain their flavor better during long cook times.

- For more flavor in soups and stews, substitute broth for the water or add bouillon cubes with the water.

- Ground red pepper (cayenne) and red pepper sauce tend to become bitter during long, slow cooking. Use small amounts, and taste during the last hour of cooking to decide whether you need to add more.

Watching the Clock

Slow cookers require little to no clock watching. For the most part, you can prepare the recipe, turn on the cooker and then forget about it until you're ready to eat. Here are some timely tips:

- A low setting is often suggested in recipes because longer cooking times fit best into workday schedules. You can fast-forward the cooking time by turning the slow cooker to high for 1 hour, which counts as 2 hours on low.

- Smaller isn't always faster. Baby-cut carrots, for example, take longer to cook than some other veggies. Remember to check for doneness.

- Slow cookers offer flexibility. Most cooked food can be held up to an hour on the low setting without overcooking. Some recipes, such as dips and spreads, can be kept on low for several hours. Be sure to stir occasionally if needed.

- Don't peek! Removing the cover allows heat to escape and adds 15 to 20 minutes to the cooking time. If you absolutely can't wait to see inside, try spinning the cover until the steam clears.

The Perfect Ending

When it comes to preparing meals in your slow cooker, the phrase "save the best for last" often applies. To get the most flavor from your slow-cooker foods, try these helpful hints:

- Develop flavors in the juices by removing the lid and cooking on the high setting for the last 20 to 30 minutes. This evaporates the water so the flavors become more intense.

- Stir in fresh herbs during the last hour of cooking so they stay flavorful. Some herbs, such as oregano and basil, change flavor with an extended cooking time.

- Fish and seafood fall apart during long hours of cooking, and some seafood, such as shrimp, becomes very tough. Add these ingredients during the last hour of cooking.

- Add tender vegetables, such as fresh tomatoes, mushrooms and zucchini, during the last 30 minutes of cooking so they don't become overcooked and mushy.

- Frozen vegetables that have been thawed will keep their bright color and crisp-tender texture if you add them during the last 30 minutes of cooking.

- Dairy products, such as milk, sour cream and cheese have a tendency to curdle. Keep sauces and gravies from "breaking down" by adding these ingredients during the last 30 minutes of cooking.

- For more texture and a little extra flavor, sprinkle the top of your slow-cooker meal with chopped fresh herbs, grated cheese, crushed croutons or corn chips, chopped tomatoes or sliced green onions just before serving.

Adapting Your Own Recipes

Want to convert a favorite range-top recipe to a slow-cooker recipe? Consider the following:

- Find a recipe in this cookbook similar to the recipe you want to adapt, and use it as a guide for quantities, amount of liquid and cooking time.

- Reduce the liquid in your recipe by about half unless you are making a soup. Liquids don't boil away as much in the slow cooker as they do in other cooking methods.

- Less-expensive meats work well in the moist heat and low temperatures of the slow cooker. Trim as much visible fat as possible from the meat before cooking so there is less to remove from the finished dish.

- Fresh dairy products, such as cheese and milk, can curdle. Add these near the end of cooking, or substitute canned condensed soups, nonfat dry milk powder or canned evaporated milk.

- Allow enough time. Most soups, stews and one-dish meals require 8 to 10 hours on the low setting.

Food-Safety Check

When using a slow cooker, keep the following list of food safety guidelines in mind:

- Begin with clean utensils, work area and slow cooker. Wash hands before and during food preparation.

- Perishable foods should be kept refrigerated until preparation time. If you cut up vegetables in advance, store them separately in the refrigerator. The slow cooker may take several hours to reach a safe, bacteria-killing temperature. Constant refrigeration assures that bacteria, which multiply rapidly at room temperature, won't get a "head start" during the first few hours of cooking.

- Thaw frozen meats and poultry completely before cooking in your slow cooker. To ensure food reaches an internal temperature of 140° within 4 hours, thaw meat and poultry in the refrigerator or microwave oven before placing it in the slow cooker.

- Ground meat should always be cooked and drained before being added to the slow cooker.

- Brown poultry and meats just before placing in your slow cooker. Bacteria can survive and grow if the food is browned the night before and then refrigerated.

- The highest setting should be used for the first hour of cooking time, if possible. Then lower the slow cooker to the setting called for in your recipe. However, it's safe to cook food on low the entire time—if you're leaving for work, for example, and preparation time is limited.

- Raw poultry and meats in a slow cooker recipe should cook a minimum of 3 hours to ensure thorough cooking.

BettyCrocker.com

- Whole chickens should not be cooked in a slow cooker because the temperature of the middle of the chicken, near the bone, cannot reach the desired level quickly enough for food safety.

- Cut meats and vegetables into the sizes specified in the recipe, and layer or assemble the ingredients as directed in the cooking method for accurate cooking times and doneness.

- Remove leftovers from the slow cooker and refrigerate or freeze as soon as you are finished eating. Cooked food shouldn't stand at room temperature longer than 2 hours before storing. Your slow cooker shouldn't be used as a storage container.

- Reheat leftovers on the stove-top or in the microwave oven rather than in your slow cooker. Heat the cooked food until thoroughly hot and then place into a preheated slow cooker to keep hot for serving.

High Altitude Tips

Cooking at high altitudes (3,500 feet and above) presents certain challenges, and slow cooking is no exception. Because no set rules apply to all recipes, trial and error is often the best way to make improvements.

- Longer cooking is necessary for most foods, particularly meats cooked in boiling liquid. The time may be up to twice as long as the recipe suggests for meats to become tender. To shorten the cooking time, try cooking meats on the high setting instead of on low.

- Cut vegetables into smaller pieces than the recipe suggests to help them cook more quickly.

- Call your local USDA (United States Department of Agriculture) Extension Service office, listed in the phone book under "county government," with questions about slow cooking at high altitudes.

Dips, Spreads & More

1

- Hot Nacho Bean Dip 12
- Smoky Bacon and Gruyère Dip 13
- Hot Artichoke and Spinach Dip 14
- Party Crab Dip 16
- Cheesy Chicken and Peppers Dip 18
- Pizza Fondue 20
- Sausage and Pepperoni Dip 22
- Asian Chicken Drummies 23
- White Chili Mini Tacos 24
- Hot Dog and Bacon Roll-Ups 25
- Mini Cheeseburger Bites 26
- French Onion Meatballs 28
- Maple-Mustard Barbecued Meatballs and Sausages 30
- Hot and Spicy Riblets 31
- Teriyaki Smoked Riblets 32
- Chex® Party Mix 34
- Spiced Party Nut Mix 35

◄ **Asian Chicken Drummies (page 23)
& Spiced Party Nut Mix (page 35)**

Hot Nacho Bean Dip

9 cups dip (36 servings)

SLOW COOKER:
3 1/2- to 4-quart

PREP TIME:
10 minutes

COOK TIME:
Low 3 to 4 hours

HOLD TIME:
Low up to 3 hours

Betty's Success Tip

If you prefer a milder-flavored bean dip, use regular process cheese spread instead. Hot or mild, tame or wild? It's your call.

Serving Suggestion

For those who can take the heat, offer sliced jalapeño chilies to sprinkle on their chips. Wear gloves when slicing the chilies because they contain caustic oils that can irritate your hands.

2 cans (16 ounces each) refried beans

2 cans (15 ounces each) black beans, rinsed and drained

1 can (4 1/2 ounces) chopped green chiles, undrained

1 envelope (1 1/4 ounces) taco seasoning mix

1 package (2 pounds) process cheese spread loaf with jalapeño peppers, cut into cubes

1 cup finely shredded Mexican cheese blend (4 ounces)

Corn chips or tortilla chips, if desired

1. Mix all ingredients except shredded cheese and corn chips in 3 1/2- to 4-quart slow cooker.

2. Cover and cook on low heat setting 3 to 4 hours, stirring after 2 hours, until cheese is melted.

3. Scrape down side of cooker with rubber spatula to help prevent edge of dip from scorching. Sprinkle with shredded cheese. Serve with corn chips. Dip will hold on low heat setting up to 3 hours.

1/4 Cup: Calories 165 (Calories from Fat 80); Fat 9g (Saturated 6g); Cholesterol 30mg; Sodium 600mg; Carbohydrate 11g (Dietary Fiber 3g); Protein 10g • **% Daily Value:** Vitamin A 8%; Vitamin C 2%; Calcium 16%; Iron 6% • **Diet Exchanges:** 1 Starch, 1 High-Fat Meat • **Carbohydrate Choices:** 1

Smoky Bacon and Gruyère Dip

3 cups dip (24 servings)

SLOW COOKER:
1 1/2-quart

PREP TIME:
10 minutes

COOK TIME:
Low 2 1/2 to 3 hours

FINISHING COOK TIME:
High 15 minutes

HOLD TIME:
Low up to 2 hours

1 clove garlic, finely chopped

1 small onion, finely chopped (1/4 cup)

1 package (8 ounces) cream cheese, cubed

2 cups shredded Gruyère cheese (8 ounces)

1 cup half-and-half

8 slices peppered smoked bacon, crisply cooked and crumbled

2 tablespoons cream-style horseradish

1/3 cup chopped fresh Italian parsley

French or herbed bread cubes or water crackers, if desired

1. Mix garlic, onion, cream cheese, Gruyère cheese and half-and-half in 1 1/2-quart slow cooker.

2. Cover and cook on low heat setting 2 hours 30 minutes to 3 hours or until mixture is hot.

3. Stir in bacon, horseradish and parsley. Cover and cook on high heat setting about 15 minutes or until mixture is hot. Scrape down side of cooker with rubber spatula to help prevent edge of dip from scorching. Turn to low heat setting to serve. Serve with bread cubes or crackers. Dip will hold on low heat setting up to 2 hours.

Ingredient Substitution

The peppered smoked bacon adds a nice peppery flavor, but regular bacon, crisply cooked and crumbled, can be used instead. The dip will still have a pleasant, smoky taste.

Serving Suggestion

Cheese and smoky bacon flavors are the perfect match for fresh vegetables. Serve this delicious dip with asparagus spears, pea pods, cauliflower flowerets, broccoli flowerets and cherry tomatoes.

2 Tablespoons: Calories 95 (Calories from Fat 70); Fat 8g (Saturated 5g); Cholesterol 25mg; Sodium 95mg; Carbohydrate 3g (Dietary Fiber 0g); Protein 4g • **% Daily Value:** Vitamin A 6%; Vitamin C 2%; Calcium 10%; Iron 0% • **Diet Exchanges:** 1/2 High-Fat Meat, 1 Fat • **Carbohydrate Choices:** 0

Hot Artichoke and Spinach Dip

2 1/2 cups dip (20 servings)

SLOW COOKER:
1- to 3-quart

PREP TIME:
15 minutes

COOK TIME:
Low 1 1/2 to 2 1/2 hours

HOLD TIME:
Low up to 4 hours

Ingredient Substitution

Swiss cheese is a natural in this dip, but experiment by using another mild cheese. Shredded mozzarella, Monterey Jack, provolone and Gouda are all great choices.

Serving Suggestion

For added flavor and texture, toast the French bread slices or serve with soft garlic bread sticks. Vegetables, such as sticks of jicama, asparagus spears, cherry tomatoes and baby carrots, also make great dippers.

2 cups frozen cut leaf spinach (from 1-pound bag)

1 can (14 ounces) quartered artichoke hearts, drained and chopped

1/2 cup refrigerated Alfredo pasta sauce (from 10-ounce container)

1/2 cup mayonnaise or salad dressing

3/4 teaspoon garlic salt

1/4 teaspoon pepper

1 cup shredded Swiss cheese (4 ounces)

French bread slices, if desired

1. Cook spinach as directed on package. Drain spinach, pressing with fork to remove excess liquid. Chop spinach finely.

2. Mix spinach and remaining ingredients except bread slices in 1- to 3-quart slow cooker.

3. Cover and cook on low heat setting 1 hour 30 minutes to 2 hours 30 minutes.

4. Scrape down side of cooker with rubber spatula to help prevent edge of dip from scorching. Serve with bread slices. Dip will hold on low heat setting up to 4 hours; stir occasionally.

2 Tablespoons: Calories 100 (Calories from Fat 70); Fat 8g (Saturated 3g); Cholesterol 15mg; Sodium 180mg; Carbohydrate 4g (Dietary Fiber 1g); Protein 3g • **% Daily Value:** Vitamin A 22%; Vitamin C 6%; Calcium 10%; Iron 2% • **Diet Exchanges:** 1/2 High-Fat Meat, 1 Fat • **Carbohydrate Choices:** 0

Hot Artichoke and Spinach Dip

Party Crab Dip

2 1/2 cups dip (24 servings)

SLOW COOKER:
1- to 3-quart

PREP TIME:
10 minutes

COOK TIME:
Low 1 1/2 to 2 1/2 hours

HOLD TIME:
Low up to 4 hours

Ingredient Substitution

Use shredded imitation crab-meat, also called surimi, if you don't have canned crabmeat on hand. Surimi is actually made from white-fleshed fish, like pollock or whiting, and can be found in the refrigerator or freezer section of your supermarket.

Finishing Touch

Spruce up this creamy dip with a sprinkle of toasted almonds. To toast almonds, heat a small skillet over medium heat. Add 3 tablespoons of sliced almonds, and cook for 1 to 2 minutes, stirring occasionally, until toasted. Sprinkle the toasted almonds over the dip just before serving.

1 package (8 ounces) cream cheese, softened

1/2 cup mayonnaise or salad dressing

1/4 cup sour cream

1 teaspoon garlic salt

2 teaspoons white wine Worcestershire sauce

1 tablespoon dry sherry or apple juice

4 medium green onions, sliced (1/4 cup)

2 cans (6 ounces each) crabmeat, drained and cartilage removed

Assorted crackers or cut-up fresh vegetables, if desired

1. Mix cream cheese, mayonnaise, sour cream, garlic salt and Worcestershire sauce in 1- to 3-quart slow cooker, using fork. Gently mix in sherry, onions and crabmeat.

2. Cover and cook on low heat setting 1 hour 30 minutes to 2 hours 30 minutes.

3. Scrape down side of cooker with rubber spatula to help prevent edge of dip from scorching. Serve with crackers or vegetables. Dip will hold on low heat setting up to 4 hours; stir occasionally.

2 Tablespoons: Calories 115 (Calories from Fat 80); Fat 9g (Saturated 4g); Cholesterol 30mg; Sodium 180mg; Carbohydrate 1g (Dietary Fiber 0g); Protein 5g • **% Daily Value:** Vitamin A 4%; Vitamin C 2%; Calcium 2%; Iron 2% • **Diet Exchanges:** 1/2 Very Lean Meat, 2 Fat • **Carbohydrate Choices:** 0

Get-Togethers

There's nothing like a slow cooker to make party-time carefree. Slow cookers make buffets a breeze to prepare and serve. So invite the gang and dig in with these crowd-pleasing menu ideas.

South-of-the-Border Bash

Cheesy Chicken and Peppers Dip (page 18)

Spicy Black Bean Barbecue Chili (page 64)

Spanish Rice with Tomatoes and Peppers (page 142)

Orange slices sprinkled with coconut

Strawberry margaritas

Decoration Ideas: Mini cacti, cut-out paper banners, straw sombrero for chips; use red, green and white napkins, streamers and tablecloth

Easy and Elegant

Smoky Bacon and Gruyère Dip (page 13)

Sherry Buttered Mushrooms (page 145)

Spinach salad with raspberry vinaigrette

Turkey Breast with Sherried Stuffing (page 70)

Chocolate truffles

Champagne

Decoration Ideas: White tea lights, silver table runner or tablecloth, white cloth napkins

Orient Express

Asian Chicken Drummies (page 23)

Asian BBQ Beef Brisket (page 106)

Jasmine rice

Bowls of peanuts and cashews

Assorted beers

Fortune cookies

Decoration Ideas: Chopsticks, bamboo plants, colorful paper lanterns, origami animals

Gone Fishin'

Party Crab Dip (page 16)

Fisherman's Wharf Seafood Stew (page 52)

Bayou Gumbo (page 46)

Fish-shaped crackers and oyster crackers

Sparkling water

Decoration Ideas: Fishing poles, straw hats with lures, blue plates and napkins, fish balloons, toy boats

Buffet Basics

The most important rule to remember when throwing a party is to have fun! When your guests see a happy and relaxed host, they can't help but have a good time.

- **Traffic Flow:** Wherever you decide to set up the buffet—the dining room table, two folding tables placed together, a kitchen counter or a picnic table—make sure traffic can flow easily around the serving area.

- **Spread Out:** Instead of one large buffet table, you may want to set up "stations" at smaller tables where guests can help themselves. To prevent traffic jams, place the main course at one table, dessert and coffee at another.

- **What's That?:** Use place cards to identify unusual foods or items that contain nuts to alert those who are allergic.

- **Stay Simmering:** To keep slow cookers plugged in during the party, push the buffet table up against a wall with an electrical outlet. Make sure cords stay tucked out of the way.

- **Full Circle:** Place the food in order so guests can serve themselves without having to backtrack. Main course goes first, then vegetables, salad, condiments and bread.

- **Useful Utensils:** Set out flatware and napkins at the end of the table so guests will have both hands free to serve themselves as they go through the line.

Cheesy Chicken and Peppers Dip

8 cups dip (32 servings)

SLOW COOKER:
3 1/2- to 4-quart

PREP TIME:
15 minutes

COOK TIME:
Low 8 to 10 hours

FINISHING COOK TIME:
Low 30 minutes

HOLD TIME:
Low up to 2 hours

Betty's Success Tip

Get an extra burst of flavor by adding 2 finely chopped chipotle chilies in adobo sauce or 2 seeded and finely chopped jalapeño chilies along with the green chiles.

Ingredient Substitution

If you don't have any red bell peppers on hand, use 2 green bell peppers instead. It may not be quite as colorful, but the dip will have the same great taste.

2 pounds boneless, skinless chicken thighs (about 10 thighs)

1 can (10 ounces) enchilada sauce

1 can (4 1/2 ounces) chopped green chiles, undrained

1 medium red bell pepper, chopped (1 cup)

1 medium green bell pepper, chopped (1 cup)

2 packages (8 ounces each) cream cheese, cut into cubes and softened

4 cups shredded Cheddar cheese (16 ounces)

Large tortilla chips, if desired

1. Place chicken, enchilada sauce and chiles in 3 1/2- to 4-quart slow cooker.

2. Cover and cook on low heat setting 8 to 10 hours or until juice of chicken is no longer pink when centers of thickest pieces are cut.

3. Stir in bell peppers, cream cheese and Cheddar cheese. Cover and cook on low heat setting about 30 minutes, stirring once or twice, until cheese is melted. Scrape down side of cooker with rubber spatula to help prevent edge of dip from scorching. Serve with tortilla chips. Dip will hold on low heat setting up to 2 hours. Stir occasionally.

1/4 Cup: Calories 250 (Calories from Fat 170); Fat 19g (Saturated 11g); Cholesterol 80mg; Sodium 310mg; Carbohydrate 3g (Dietary Fiber 1g); Protein 18g • **% Daily Value:** Vitamin A 24%; Vitamin C 20%; Calcium 12%; Iron 10% • **Diet Exchanges:** 3 Medium-Fat Meat • **Carbohydrate Choices:** 0

Cheesy Chicken and Peppers Dip

Pizza Fondue

3 1/2 cups fondue (14 servings)

SLOW COOKER:
1 1/2-quart

PREP TIME:
20 minutes

COOK TIME:
Low 3 to 4 hours

HOLD TIME:
Low up to 2 hours

Betty's Success Tip

The fondue may thicken, so check it occasionally. If it becomes too thick, stir in a small amount of hot water until it's the desired consistency for dipping.

Serving Suggestion

Turn this zesty dip into a pizza party by serving it with cubes of focaccia or toasted garlic bread along with the vegetables for dipping.

1 jar (14 ounces) pizza sauce

1 cup chopped turkey pepperoni (from 6-ounce package)

8 medium green onions, chopped (1/2 cup)

1/2 cup chopped red bell pepper

1 can (2 1/4 ounces) sliced ripe olives, drained

1 cup shredded mozzarella cheese (4 ounces)

1 package (8 ounces) cream cheese, softened and cubed

Broccoli flowerets, cherry tomatoes and carrot sticks, if desired

1. Mix pizza sauce, pepperoni, onions, bell pepper and olives in 1 1/2-quart slow cooker.

2. Cover and cook on low heat setting 3 to 4 hours or until mixture is hot.

3. Stir in mozzarella cheese and cream cheese until melted. Scrape down side of cooker with rubber spatula to help prevent edge of dip from scorching. Serve with vegetables. Dip will hold on low heat setting up to 2 hours. Stir occasionally.

1/4 Cup: Calories 135 (Calories from Fat 110); Fat 12g (Saturated 6g); Cholesterol 35mg; Sodium 320mg; Carbohydrate 3g (Dietary Fiber 1g); Protein 5g • **% Daily Value:** Vitamin A 14%; Vitamin C 10%; Calcium 8%; Iron 4% • **Diet Exchanges:** 1 High-Fat Meat, 1 Fat • **Carbohydrate Choices:** 0

Pizza Fondue

Sausage and Pepperoni Dip

3 1/2 cups dip (28 servings)

SLOW COOKER:
1 1/2- to 3-quart

PREP TIME:
15 minutes

COOK TIME:
Low 2 to 3 hours

HOLD TIME:
Low up to 2 hours

3/4 pound bulk Italian pork sausage

1/3 cup chopped onion

1/2 cup sliced pepperoni (2 ounces), chopped

1/4 cup ketchup

1 jar (14 ounces) pizza sauce

2 cups shredded mozzarella cheese (8 ounces)

Baguette-style French bread slices or assorted crackers, if desired

Ingredient Substitution

A tomato pasta sauce can be used instead of the pizza sauce to vary the flavor. Garden vegetable or mushroom and ripe olive also add bits of veggies to the dip.

Finishing Touch

Who doesn't love the stringy cheese of warm pizza! For that cheesy experience, sprinkle the top of this zesty Italian dip with additional shredded mozzarella cheese just before serving.

1. Cook sausage and onion in 10-inch skillet over medium-high heat, stirring frequently, until sausage is no longer pink; drain. Stir in pepperoni, ketchup and pizza sauce.

2. Spray 1 1/2- to 3-quart slow cooker with cooking spray. Spoon sausage mixture into cooker. Stir in cheese.

3. Cover and cook on low heat setting 2 to 3 hours or until cheese is melted and mixture is hot.

4. Scrape down side of cooker with rubber spatula to help prevent edge of dip from scorching. Serve with bread or crackers. Dip will hold on low heat setting up to 2 hours. Stir occasionally.

2 Tablespoons: Calories 75 (Calories from Fat 45); Fat 5g (Saturated 2g); Cholesterol 15mg; Sodium 260mg; Carbohydrate 2g (Dietary Fiber 0g); Protein 5g • **% Daily Value:** Vitamin A 2%; Vitamin C 2%; Calcium 6%; Iron 2% • **Diet Exchanges:** 1/2 High-Fat Meat • **Carbohydrate Choices:** 0

Asian Chicken Drummies

28 appetizers

Photo on page 10

SLOW COOKER:
4- to 6-quart

PREP TIME:
10 minutes

BAKE TIME:
45 minutes

COOK TIME:
Low 1 to 2 hours

HOLD TIME:
Low up to 2 hours

Betty's Success Tip

Hoisin sauce is often used in Chinese cuisine. The reddish brown sauce, flavored with soybeans, garlic, chili peppers and numerous spices, tastes spicy and sweet.

Ingredient Substitution

Chicken drummettes are chicken wings trimmed to resemble small chicken legs. If you're having trouble finding drummettes, you can make your own by using chicken wings. Cut off and discard the tips, then cut the wings through the joint into two pieces. To shape tiny drumsticks, push the meat and skin to one end of the bone, leaving the bone exposed so it resembles a chicken drumstick.

1 package (3 pounds) frozen chicken drummettes, thawed

3 tablespoons butter or margarine, melted

1/4 cup all-purpose flour

1/3 cup hoisin sauce

2 tablespoons oriental chili-garlic sauce or chili puree with garlic

1. Heat oven to 450°. Pat excess moisture from thawed drummettes, using paper towels; place drummettes in large bowl. Drizzle 2 tablespoons of the melted butter over drummettes. Sprinkle with flour; toss to mix. (Mixture will be crumbly.)

2. Arrange drummettes in single layer in ungreased rectangular pan, 15 1/2 × 10 1/2 × 1 inch. Bake 40 to 45 minutes or until crisp and brown.

3. Transfer browned drummettes to 4- to 6-quart slow cooker, using slotted spoon. Mix remaining 1 tablespoon butter, the hoisin sauce and chili-garlic sauce. Pour over drummettes; toss lightly to coat.

4. Cover and cook on low heat setting 1 to 2 hours or until juice of drummettes is no longer pink when centers of thickest pieces are cut. Drummettes will hold on low heat setting up to 2 hours.

1 Appetizer: Calories 75 (Calories from Fat 45); Fat 5g (Saturated 2g); Cholesterol 20mg; Sodium 85mg; Carbohydrate 2g (Dietary Fiber 0g); Protein 5g • **% Daily Value:** Vitamin A 2%; Vitamin C 0%; Calcium 0%; Iron 0% • **Diet Exchanges:** 1 Medium Fat-Meat • **Carbohydrate Choices:** 0

White Chili Mini Tacos

48 appetizers

SLOW COOKER:
4- to 6-quart

PREP TIME:
5 minutes

COOK TIME:
Low 5 to 6 hours

HOLD TIME:
Low up to 3 hours

Betty's Success Tip

For a fun Mexican party buffet, pile warm mini taco shells on a platter lined with napkins in festive colors. Set out bowls of taco toppings around the slow cooker filled with the chicken mixture.

Ingredient Substitution

Provide warm small flour tortillas for those who prefer soft-shell tacos. To warm tortillas, wrap them in aluminum foil and heat in a 325° oven for about 15 minutes. Or place on a microwavable paper towel and microwave on High for 30 seconds.

1 1/4 pounds boneless, skinless chicken thighs (about 6 thighs)

2 tablespoons taco seasoning mix (from 1 1/4-ounce envelope)

1 can (4 1/2 ounces) chopped green chiles, undrained

1 can (19 ounces) cannellini beans, drained

2 packages (3.8 ounces each) miniature taco shells (48 shells)

1. Place chicken thighs in 4- to 6-quart slow cooker; sprinkle with taco seasoning mix. Top with chiles and beans.

2. Cover and cook on low heat setting 5 to 6 hours or until juice of chicken is no longer pink when the centers of the thickest pieces are cut.

3. About 15 minutes before serving, heat taco shells as directed on package. Meanwhile, remove chicken from cooker; place on large plate. Shred chicken with 2 forks. Return chicken to bean mixture; mix well, mashing beans with fork.

4. Serve chicken mixture with warm taco shells. Chicken mixture will hold on low heat setting up to 3 hours.

1 Appetizer: Calories 55 (Calories from Fat 20); Fat 2g (Saturated 0g); Cholesterol 5mg; Sodium 55mg; Carbohydrate 6g (Dietary Fiber 1g); Protein 4g • **% Daily Value:** Vitamin A 0%; Vitamin C 0%; Calcium 2%; Iron 4% • **Diet Exchanges:** 1/2 Starch, 1/2 Very Lean Meat • **Carbohydrate Choices:** 1/2

Hot Dog and Bacon Roll-Ups

40 appetizers

SLOW COOKER:
3 1/2- to 4-quart

PREP TIME:
20 minutes

COOK TIME:
High 4 hours

HOLD TIME:
Low up to 2 hours

Betty's Success Tip

The process of heating sugar until it liquefies and becomes syrup is called caramelization. The sweet and slightly spicy sauce that's made from the sugar and seasonings also crisps the bacon in these flavorful, fun roll-ups.

Serving Suggestion

Kids will love these hot dogs with their sweet and salty combination of sugar and bacon. Serve these little treats at a birthday party, and you're guaranteed grins all around.

2 cups packed brown sugar

1 teaspoon ground mustard

1/2 teaspoon garlic powder

1 tablespoon chili powder

2 packages (1 pound each) hot dogs, cut crosswise in half

20 slices bacon (about 1 1/2 pounds), cut crosswise in half

1. Mix brown sugar, mustard, garlic powder and chili powder in small bowl.

2. Wrap each hot dog half with a half slice of bacon; secure with toothpick. Arrange a layer of roll-ups in bottom of 3 1/2- to 4-quart slow cooker. Sprinkle one-third of the sugar mixture on top. Repeat layering roll-ups and sugar mixture 2 more times, ending with sugar mixture.

3. Cover and cook on high heat setting about 4 hours, gently stirring twice, until bacon is crisp. Turn to low heat setting to serve. Roll-ups will hold on low heat setting up to 2 hours.

1 Appetizer: Calories 130 (Calories from Fat 70); Fat 8g (Saturated 3g); Cholesterol 15mg; Sodium 330mg; Carbohydrate 12g (Dietary Fiber 0g); Protein 3g • **% Daily Value:** Vitamin A 2%; Vitamin C 0%; Calcium 0%; Iron 2% • **Diet Exchanges:** 1 Fruit, 1/2 Lean Meat, 1 Fat • **Carbohydrate Choices:** 1

Mini Cheeseburger Bites

24 appetizers

SLOW COOKER:
3 1/2- to 4-quart

PREP TIME:
15 minutes

COOK TIME:
Low 3 to 4 hours

HOLD TIME:
Low up to 3 hours

Ingredient Substitution

To add a little zip to these mini burgers, use Monterey Jack cheese with jalapeño peppers instead of American cheese.

Serving Suggestion

For a kid's birthday party, spoon the meat mixture on small round bun halves. Let kids decorate their own open-face sandwiches with ketchup and mustard in squeeze containers. Set out bowls of shredded cheese, sliced pickles, cherry tomato halves and sliced olives so they can make silly faces.

1 pound lean ground beef

2 tablespoons ketchup

2 teaspoons instant minced onion

1 teaspoon yellow mustard

8 ounces American cheese, cut into 2-inch cubes (2 cups)

24 miniature sandwich buns, split

1. Cook beef in 10-inch skillet over medium-high heat about 8 minutes, stirring frequently, until brown; drain. Stir in ketchup, onion and mustard.

2. Spray 3 1/2- to 4-quart slow cooker with cooking spray. Spoon beef mixture into cooker. Top with cheese.

3. Cover and cook on low heat setting 3 to 4 hours or until mixture is hot and cheese is melted.

4. Serve beef mixture with buns. Beef mixture will hold on low heat setting up to 3 hours.

1 Appetizer: Calories 165 (Calories from Fat 70); Fat 8g (Saturated 3g); Cholesterol 20mg; Sodium 310mg; Carbohydrate 15g (Dietary Fiber 1g); Protein 8g • **% Daily Value:** Vitamin A 2%; Vitamin C 0%; Calcium 8%; Iron 6% • **Diet Exchanges:** 1 Starch, 1/2 High-Fat Meat, 1/2 Fat • **Carbohydrate Choices:** 1

Mini Cheeseburger Bites

French Onion Meatballs

72 appetizers

SLOW COOKER:
4- to 6-quart

PREP TIME:
5 minutes

COOK TIME:
Low 3 1/2 to 4 1/2 hours

HOLD TIME:
Low up to 2 hours

2 packages (18 ounces each) frozen cooked meatballs

1 jar (12 ounces) beef gravy

1/2 package (2-ounce size) onion soup mix (1 envelope)

1 tablespoon dry sherry, if desired

1. Place meatballs in 4- to 6-quart slow cooker. Mix gravy, soup mix (dry) and sherry in medium bowl. Pour over meatballs; stir gently to mix.

2. Cover and cook on low heat setting 3 hours 30 minutes to 4 hours 30 minutes or until meatballs are hot. Meatballs will hold on low heat setting up to 2 hours.

Betty's Success Tip

If you have a favorite recipe for meatballs, use it instead of the frozen meatballs. Simply shape the meatball mixture into 72 appetizer-size balls. Cook the meatballs thoroughly, then combine them with the sauce ingredients in the slow cooker.

Serving Suggestion

You can turn this easy appetizer into a satisfying meal. Serve the meatballs over egg noodles, rice or couscous and sprinkle with chopped parsley. Add steamed green beans and a salad of fresh sliced tomatoes drizzled with olive oil and sprinkled with shredded or shaved Parmesan cheese.

1 Appetizer: Calories 45 (Calories from Fat 25); Fat 3g (Saturated 1g); Cholesterol 15mg; Sodium 120mg; Carbohydrate 2g (Dietary Fiber 0g); Protein 3g • **% Daily Value:** Vitamin A 0%; Vitamin C 0%; Calcium 0%; Iron 2% • **Diet Exchanges:** 1/2 High-Fat Meat • **Carbohydrate Choices:** 0

French Onion Meatballs

Maple-Mustard Barbecued Meatballs and Sausages

28 appetizers

SLOW COOKER:
3 1/2- to 4-quart

PREP TIME:
8 minutes

COOK TIME:
High 3 hours

HOLD TIME:
Low up to 2 hours

Ingredient Substitution

Cocktail sausages and meatballs are both easy and popular appetizers. Now you can serve them together in one simple dish. If you prefer just cocktail sausages or meatballs, use 2 packages of either one instead of combining them.

Serving Suggestion

This easy appetizer is perfect fare for a football play-off party. Provide napkins and plates to match the team colors, and you'll wind up a winner—no matter what the final score is!

1 package (16 ounces) cocktail sausages

1 package (18 ounces) frozen cooked meatballs

1 bottle (18 ounces) barbecue sauce

1 cup maple-flavored syrup

3 tablespoons spicy brown mustard

1. Mix all ingredients in 3 1/2- to 4-quart slow cooker.

2. Cover and cook on high heat setting about 3 hours, gently stirring after 2 hours, until hot.

3. Turn to low heat setting to serve. Serve with large serving spoon. Appetizers will hold on low heat setting up to 2 hours.

1 Appetizer: Calories 220 (Calories from Fat 90); Fat 9g (Saturated 4g); Cholesterol 40mg; Sodium 670mg; Carbohydrate 25g (Dietary Fiber 0g); Protein 7g • **% Daily Value:** Vitamin A 2%; Vitamin C 0%; Calcium 8%; Iron 6% • **Diet Exchanges:** 1 1/2 Starch, 1/2 High-Fat Meat, 1 Fat • **Carbohydrate Choices:** 1 1/2

Hot and Spicy Riblets
About 30 appetizers

SLOW COOKER:
3 1/2- to 4-quart

PREP TIME:
10 minutes

COOK TIME:
Low 6 to 7 hours

FINISHING COOK TIME:
High 25 to 30 minutes

HOLD TIME:
Low up to 2 hours

1 rack (3 pounds) pork back ribs, cut lengthwise across bones in half, then cut into 1-rib pieces

3 cloves garlic, finely chopped

1 cup ketchup

1/4 cup packed brown sugar

1/4 cup chopped chipotle chiles in adobo sauce (from 7-ounce can)

1 tablespoon cider vinegar

1 tablespoon Worcestershire sauce

1 teaspoon salt

Betty's Success Tip

For these smaller, party-sized pieces, be sure to ask your butcher to cut the ribs lengthwise across the bones, then crosswise into one-rib pieces.

Ingredient Substitution

Out of fresh garlic? Check your spice rack. One medium clove of garlic is equal to 1/8 teaspoon garlic powder or 1/4 teaspoon instant minced garlic.

1. Spray 3 1/2- to 4-quart slow cooker with cooking spray. Place riblets in cooker. Sprinkle with garlic.

2. Cover and cook on low heat setting 6 to 7 hours or until ribs are tender.

3. About 35 minutes before serving, mix remaining ingredients in 2–cup glass measuring cup or small bowl. Drain and discard juices from cooker. Pour or spoon sauce over riblets, stirring gently to coat evenly. Increase heat setting to high; cover and cook 25 to 30 minutes or until riblets are glazed.

4. Turn to low heat setting to serve. Riblets will hold on low heat setting up to 2 hours.

1 Appetizer: Calories 105 (Calories from Fat 65); Fat 7g (Saturated 2g); Cholesterol 25mg; Sodium 220mg; Carbohydrate 4g (Dietary Fiber 0g); Protein 7g • **% Daily Value:** Vitamin A 2%; Vitamin C 0%; Calcium 0%; Iron 2% • **Diet Exchanges:** 1 High-Fat Meat • **Carbohydrate Choices:** 0

Teriyaki Smoked Riblets

About 30 appetizers

SLOW COOKER:
3 1/2- to 4-quart

PREP TIME:
10 minutes

COOK TIME:
Low 6 to 8 hours

HOLD TIME:
Low up to 2 hours

1 rack (3 pounds) smoked pork back ribs, cut lengthwise across bones in half, then cut into 1-rib pieces

3/4 cup ketchup

1/2 cup pineapple preserves

1/2 cup teriyaki marinade and sauce (from 11-ounce bottle)

1/4 cup packed brown sugar

2 cloves garlic, finely chopped

1. Spray inside of 3 1/2- to 4-quart slow cooker with cooking spray. Place riblets in cooker. Mix remaining ingredients; pour over ribs.

2. Cover and cook on low heat setting 6 to 8 hours or until ribs are tender. Skim fat if necessary. Riblets will hold on low heat setting up to 2 hours.

Betty's Success Tip

It's easy to remove the fat after the ribs are cooked. Either use a spoon and skim the surface of the sauce or place a slice or two of bread on top of the ribs for a few minutes to soak up excess fat.

Ingredient Substitution

If smoked pork back ribs aren't available, go ahead and use regular pork back ribs instead. If you still want that smoky flavor, rub the ribs with smoke seasoning or add a few drops of liquid smoke to the sauce. You'll find the smoke seasoning in the spice aisle and the liquid smoke in the barbecue and steak sauce section of the supermarket.

1 Appetizer: Calories 110 (Calories from Fat 65); Fat 7g (Saturated 2g); Cholesterol 10mg; Sodium 430mg; Carbohydrate 8g (Dietary Fiber 0); Protein 4g • **% Daily Value:** Vitamin A 0%; Vitamin C 0%; Calcium 0%; Iron 4% • **Diet Exchanges:** 1/2 Medium-Fat Meat, 1/2 Fruit, 1 Fat • **Carbohydrate Choices:** 1/2

Teriyaki Smoked Riblets

Chex® Party Mix

12 cups (24 servings)

SLOW COOKER:
5- to 6-quart

PREP TIME:
10 minutes

COOK TIME:
Low 3 to 4 hours

Betty's Success Tip

After the slow cooker is turned off, the mix will stay warm. However, be sure to stir it every 30 minutes to prevent the pieces on the bottom from becoming too brown. Or, to free up your slow cooker, make the mix ahead and serve at room temperature. It will stay fresh up to 2 weeks stored in an airtight container.

Ingredient Substitution

This popular party mix is great as is, but you may want to add a personal touch. Use your favorite nuts for the peanuts, or eliminate the peanuts altogether and double up on the pretzels instead.

6 tablespoons butter or margarine, melted

2 tablespoons Worcestershire sauce

1/2 teaspoon garlic powder

1/2 teaspoon onion powder

1/4 teaspoon red pepper sauce

3 cups Corn Chex® cereal

3 cups Rice Chex® cereal

3 cups Wheat Chex® cereal

1 cup peanuts

1 cup pretzels

1 cup garlic-flavor bite-size bagel chips or regular-size bagel chips, broken into 1-inch pieces

1. Mix butter, Worcestershire sauce, garlic powder, onion powder and pepper sauce in 5- to 6-quart slow cooker. Gradually stir in remaining ingredients until evenly coated.

2. Cook uncovered on low heat setting 3 to 4 hours, stirring every 30 minutes, until mix is warm and flavors are blended.

3. Turn off cooker. Serve with large serving spoon.

1/2 Cup: Calories 155 (Calories from Fat 65); Fat 7g (Saturated 2g); Cholesterol 10mg; Sodium 310mg; Carbohydrate 21g (Dietary Fiber 2g); Protein 4g • **% Daily Value:** Vitamin A 2%; Vitamin C 2%; Calcium 4%; Iron 28% • **Diet Exchanges:** 1 1/2 Starch, 1 Fat • **Carbohydrate Choices:** 1 1/2

Spiced Party Nut Mix

13 cups (26 servings)

Photo on page 10

SLOW COOKER:
3 1/2- to 4-quart

PREP TIME:
15 minutes

COOK TIME:
Low 3 to 4 hours

Betty's Success Tip

Look for the pecan halves, roasted unsalted cashews, walnut halves and unblanched whole almonds in the bulk-foods section of your supermarket. Purchasing the nuts in bulk allows you to buy exactly the amount you need.

Serving Suggestion

This nut mix is best served warm, but is also tasty served at room temperature. Make it up to 2 weeks ahead and store in an airtight container at room temperature.

6 tablespoons butter or margarine, melted

1 envelope (1 1/4 ounces) taco seasoning mix

1 teaspoon ground cinnamon

1/4 teaspoon ground red pepper (cayenne)

2 cups pecan halves

2 cups roasted unsalted cashews

2 cups walnut halves

2 cups unblanched whole almonds

3 cups small cheese snack crackers

2 cups sourdough pretzel nuggets

1. Mix butter, taco seasoning mix, cinnamon and red pepper in 3 1/2- to 4-quart slow cooker. Gently toss with remaining ingredients.

2. Cook uncovered on low heat setting 3 to 4 hours, stirring every 30 minutes, until nuts are toasted.

3. Turn off cooker. Serve with large serving spoon.

1/2 Cup: Calories 320 (Calories from Fat 235); Fat 26g (Saturated 5g); Cholesterol 10mg; Sodium 200mg; Carbohydrate 15g (Dietary Fiber 3g); Protein 7g • **% Daily Value:** Vitamin A 4%; Vitamin C 0%; Calcium 6%; Iron 10% • **Diet Exchanges:** 1 Starch, 1/2 High-Fat Meat, 4 Fat • **Carbohydrate Choices:** 1

Soups, Stews & Chilies

2

- Barley-Vegetable Soup 38
- Creamy Chicken and Wild Rice Soup 39
- Creamy Split Pea Soup 40
- Two-Bean Minestrone 42
- Meatball Stone Soup 44
- Bayou Gumbo 46
- Pork Tortilla Soup 47
- Black-Eyed Pea and Sausage Soup 48
- Smoky Ham and Navy Bean Stew 49
- Chicken and Vegetable Tortellini Stew 50
- Fisherman's Wharf Seafood Stew 52
- Mexican Beef Stew 54
- Scottish Lamb Stew 56
- Curried Pork Stew 58
- Vegetable Beef Stew 60
- White Chili with Chicken 61
- Chunky Chicken Chili with Hominy 62
- Mexican Beef Chili 63
- Spicy Black Bean Barbecue Chili 64

◀ **Bayou Gumbo (page 46)**

Barley-Vegetable Soup

10 servings

SLOW COOKER:
5- to 6-quart

PREP TIME:
25 minutes

COOK TIME:
Low 6 to 8 hours

FINISHING COOK TIME:
Low 10 minutes

Betty's Success Tip

Stirring in the tomatoes at the end of the cooking time helps them maintain their texture and adds a fresher tomato flavor.

Finishing Touch

Instead of serving bread or rolls, top this warming vegetable soup with a handful of herb-flavored croutons and a little shredded Parmesan cheese. Finish the meal with a selection of fresh fruit.

1 cup uncooked barley

1 dried bay leaf

1/2 teaspoon fennel seed

1 1/2 cups baby-cut carrots, cut crosswise in half

2 medium stalks celery, sliced (1 cup)

1 medium onion, chopped (1/2 cup)

1 small green bell pepper, chopped (1/2 cup)

2 cloves garlic, finely chopped

1 large dark-orange sweet potato, peeled and cubed (2 cups)

1 1/2 cups frozen whole kernel corn (from 1-pound bag)

1 1/2 cups frozen cut green beans (from 1-pound bag)

1 1/4 teaspoons salt

1/4 teaspoon pepper

2 cans (14 ounces each) vegetable broth

6 cups water

1 can (14 1/2 ounces) diced tomatoes with herbs, undrained

1. Layer all ingredients except broth, water and tomatoes in order listed in 5- to 6–quart slow cooker. Pour broth and water over ingredients; do not stir.

2. Cover and cook on low heat setting 6 to 8 hours or until barley is tender.

3. About 10 minutes before serving, stir tomatoes into soup. Cover and cook on low heat setting about 10 minutes or until thoroughly heated. Remove bay leaf.

1 Serving: Calories 135 (Calories from Fat 10); Fat 1g (Saturated 0g); Cholesterol 0mg; Sodium 730mg; Carbohydrate 32g (Dietary Fiber 6g); Protein 4g • **% Daily Value:** Vitamin A 100%; Vitamin C 16%; Calcium 4%; Iron 6% • **Diet Exchanges:** 2 Starch, 1 Vegetable • **Carbohydrate Choices:** 2

Creamy Chicken and Wild Rice Soup

8 servings

SLOW COOKER:
3 1/2- to 4-quart

PREP TIME:
12 minutes

COOK TIME:
Low 7 to 8 hours

FINISHING COOK TIME:
High 15 to 30 minutes

Betty's Success Tip

Love this soup but want to trim the fat and calories? Reduce the calories to 230 and the fat to 7 grams per serving by using a 12-ounce can of evaporated low-fat milk instead of the half-and-half.

Ingredient Substitution

If you prefer, use a pound of boneless, skinless chicken breasts for the thighs. And if your chicken broth doesn't have roasted garlic, just stir 1/4 teaspoon garlic powder into the regular chicken broth.

1 pound boneless, skinless chicken thighs (5 thighs),
   cut into 1-inch pieces

1/2 cup uncooked wild rice

1/4 cup fresh or frozen chopped onions (from 12-ounce bag)

2 cans (10 3/4 ounces each) condensed cream of potato soup

1 can (14 ounces) chicken broth with roasted garlic

2 cups frozen sliced carrots (from 1-pound bag)

1 cup half-and-half

1. Place chicken in 3 1/2- to 4-quart slow cooker. Mix wild rice, onions, soup, broth and carrots; pour over chicken.

2. Cover and cook on low heat setting 7 to 8 hours or until chicken is no longer pink in center.

3. Stir in half-and-half. Cover and cook on high heat setting 15 to 30 minutes or until hot.

1 Serving: Calories 240 (Calories from Fat 90); Fat 10g (Saturated 4g); Cholesterol 50mg; Sodium 840mg; Carbohydrate 24g (Dietary Fiber 3g); Protein 17g • **% Daily Value:** Vitamin A 100%; Vitamin C 2%; Calcium 8%; Iron 10% • **Diet Exchanges:** 1 Starch, 1 1/2 Medium-Fat Meat, 2 Vegetable • **Carbohydrate Choices:** 1 1/2

Creamy Split Pea Soup

8 servings

SLOW COOKER:
3 1/2- to 4-quart

PREP TIME:
20 minutes

COOK TIME:
Low 10 to 11 hours

FINISHING COOK TIME:
Low 30 minutes

Betty's Success Tip

This meatless pea soup is a twist on the traditional soup made with a ham bone. If you prefer your soup with a bit of smoky flavor, just add 1 cup diced fully cooked smoked ham with the peas and reduce the salt to 1 teaspoon.

Ingredient Substitution

If you have it on hand, you can use a 48-ounce can of chicken broth and 2 cups of water instead of the 6 cups of water. You can also substitute 2 cups peeled and cubed butternut squash for the sweet potato.

2 cups dried green split peas, sorted and rinsed

6 cups water

1/2 cup dry sherry or apple juice

1 large dark-orange sweet potato, peeled and cubed (2 cups)

1 large onion, chopped (1 cup)

4 cloves garlic, finely chopped

2 teaspoons salt

3 cups firmly packed chopped fresh spinach leaves

1 cup whipping (heavy) cream

2 tablespoons chopped fresh dill weed

Freshly ground pepper to taste

1. Mix split peas, water, sherry, sweet potato, onion, garlic and salt in 3 1/2- to 4-quart slow cooker.

2. Cover and cook on low heat setting 10 to 11 hours or until peas and vegetables are tender.

3. Stir in spinach, whipping cream and dill weed. Cover and cook on low heat setting about 30 minutes or until spinach is wilted. Season with pepper.

1 Serving: Calories 235 (Calories from Fat 90); Fat 10g (Saturated 6g); Cholesterol 35mg; Sodium 910mg; Carbohydrate 35g (Dietary Fiber 11g); Protein 12g • **% Daily Value:** Vitamin A 98%; Vitamin C 8%; Calcium 6%; Iron 10% • **Diet Exchanges:** 2 Starch, 1 Vegetable, 1 Fruit • **Carbohydrate Choices:** 2

Creamy Split Pea Soup

Two-Bean Minestrone

6 servings

SLOW COOKER:
3 1/2- to 4-quart

PREP TIME:
10 minutes

COOK TIME:
Low 8 to 10 hours

FINISHING COOK TIME:
Low 15 minutes

Betty's Success Tip

Traditional pesto is a mixture of basil, garlic, olive oil and pine nuts. Check out all the pesto variations, such as sun-dried tomato, roasted bell pepper and spinach pesto, that would also make delicious toppings for this veggie-filled soup.

Ingredient Substitution

There are many shapes of pasta available so use any short-cut pasta in place of the elbow macaroni. For a different "twist" try rotini, gemelli or fusilli.

1 can (15 1/2 ounces) dark red kidney beans, drained

1 can (15 ounces) garbanzo beans, drained

1 bag (1 pound) frozen mixed vegetables

1 can (14 1/2 ounces) diced tomatoes with basil, garlic and oregano, undrained

1 large vegetarian vegetable bouillon cube

1 can (11 1/2 ounces) vegetable juice

1 cup water

1/2 cup uncooked elbow macaroni

1 container (7 ounces) refrigerated basil pesto

1. Mix all ingredients except macaroni and pesto in 3 1/2- to 4-quart slow cooker.

2. Cover and cook on low heat setting 8 to 10 hours or until vegetables are tender.

3. Stir in macaroni. Cover and cook on low heat setting about 15 minutes or until macaroni is tender. Top each serving with spoonful of pesto.

1 Serving: Calories 425 (Calories from Fat 180); Fat 20g (Saturated 4g); Cholesterol 5mg; Sodium 1040mg; Carbohydrate 56g (Dietary Fiber 15g); Protein 20g • **% Daily Value:** Vitamin A 68%; Vitamin C 44%; Calcium 24%; Iron 36% • **Diet Exchanges:** 3 1/2 Starch, 1 High-Fat Meat, 1 Fat • **Carbohydrate Choices:** 4

Easy Homemade Breads

Freshly baked bread, warm from the oven—there's no better accompaniment to slow cooker meals. Here are some quick-to-fix Bisquick breads to match up with your slow cooker favorites.

Butter Biscuits

Heat oven to 450°. Cut 1/3 cup firm butter into 1/4-inch pieces; toss with 2 1/2 cups Original Bisquick® mix with fork until coated. Add 2/3 cup milk and stir just until milk is absorbed. Place dough on surface dusted with Bisquick mix and gently roll to coat. Knead 5 times; pat lightly to 1/2-inch thickness. Cut with 3-inch cutter dipped in Bisquick mix. Place on ungreased cookie sheet with sides touching. Bake about 9 minutes or until golden brown. Brush with melted butter if desired. Serve warm. *8 biscuits.*

Try with: Two-Bean Minestrone (page 42) or Meatball Stone Soup (page 44).

Quick Corn Bread Sticks

Heat oven to 450°. Grease bottom and sides of 2 loaf pans, 9 × 5 × 3 inches, with shortening. Beat 2 eggs in large bowl with hand beater or wire whisk until fluffy. Beat in 1 cup Orginial Bisquick mix, 1 cup yellow corn-meal, 1 1/2 cups buttermilk and 2 tablespoons oil just until smooth (do not overbeat). Pour into pans. Sprinkle lightly with additional cornmeal. Bake about 15 minutes or until toothpick inserted in center comes out clean. Remove from pans. Cut each loaf crosswise into 8 sticks. Serve warm. *16 corn bread sticks.*

Try with: Chunky Chicken Chili with Hominy (page 62) or Mexican Beef Chili (page 63).

Quick French Onion Biscuits

Heat oven to 450°. Stir 2 cups Original Bisquick mix, 1/4 cup milk and 1 container (8 ounces) French onion dip until soft dough forms. Drop dough into 6 mounds onto ungreased cookie sheet. Bake 10 to 12 minutes or until light golden brown. Serve warm. *6 biscuits.*

Try with: Creamy Split Pea Soup (page 40) or Scottish Lamb Stew (page 56).

Triple-Cheese Flatbread

Heat oven to 450°. Stir 2 cups Original Bisquick mix and 1/2 cup hot water until stiff dough forms. Let stand 10 minutes. Place dough on surface sprinkled with Bisquick mix; gently roll in Bisquick mix to coat. Shape into a ball; knead 60 times. Roll or pat dough into 12-inch square on ungreased cookie sheet. Spread 2 tablespoons melted butter or margarine over dough. Mix 1/4 cup each shredded Cheddar, shredded Monterey Jack and grated Parmesan cheese; sprinkle over dough. Bake 10 to 12 minutes or until edges are golden brown. Serve warm. *16 servings.*

Try with: Vegetable Beef Stew (page 60) or Black-Eyed Pea and Sausage Soup (page 48).

Bread on the Side

In a rush? Round out your meal with these easy ideas instead.

- **Dropped biscuits** with butter or honey
- **Garlic bread** sprinkled with chopped parsley or oregano
- **Pita** or toast triangles spread with savory-flavored cream cheese
- **Breadsticks**, plain, herbed or Parmesan cheese

- **Flour tortillas** sprinkled with Monterey Jack cheese, melted and rolled
- **English muffins** or crumpets, toasted, and sprinkled with shredded Parmesan cheese
- **Pizza crust shell**, heated and cut into wedges

Meatball Stone Soup

6 servings

SLOW COOKER:
3 1/2- to 4-quart

PREP TIME:
10 minutes

COOK TIME:
Low 9 to 11 hours

FINISHING COOK TIME:
High 1 hour

Betty's Success Tip

This delicious soup borrows its name from *Stone Soup*, a children's book about a group of townspeople who share ingredients from their cupboards—including a stone!—to make a pot of soup. This slow-cooker version doesn't include the stone, but you may have all the ingredients in your freezer and pantry for those times when you don't have time to shop.

Serving Suggestion

Kids will love this soup based on the name alone! Enjoy it as an easy dinner with whole-grain rolls or bread, a large glass of cold milk and a juicy red apple.

1 bag (16 ounces) frozen Italian-style meatballs

2 cans (14 ounces each) beef broth

2 cans (14 1/2 ounces each) diced tomatoes with Italian herbs, undrained

1 medium potato, chopped (1 cup)

1 medium onion, chopped (1/2 cup)

1/4 teaspoon garlic pepper

1 bag (1 pound) frozen mixed vegetables

Shredded Parmesan cheese, if desired

1. Mix frozen meatballs, broth, tomatoes, potato, onion and garlic pepper in 3 1/2- to 4-quart slow cooker.

2. Cover and cook on low heat setting 9 to 11 hours or until vegetables are tender.

3. Stir in frozen mixed vegetables. Cover and cook on high heat setting 1 hour. Serve with Parmesan cheese.

1 Serving: Calories 425 (Calories from Fat 190); Fat 21g (Saturated 8g); Cholesterol 125mg; Sodium 1930mg; Carbohydrate 36g (Dietary Fiber 7g); Protein 30g • **% Daily Value:** Vitamin A 80%; Vitamin C 58%; Calcium 18%; Iron 28% • **Diet Exchanges:** 1 1/2 Starch, 3 Medium-Fat Meat, 2 Vegetable • **Carbohydrate Choices:** 2 1/2

Meatball Stone Soup

Bayou Gumbo

6 servings

Photo on page 36

SLOW COOKER:
3 1/2- to 4-quart

PREP TIME:
30 minutes

COOK TIME:
Low 7 to 9 hours

FINISHING COOK TIME:
Low 20 minutes

Betty's Success Tip

Okra is a signature ingredient for gumbo. The vegetable, which is popular in the South, adds flavor and helps thicken the sauce. The name gumbo actually is a derivation of the African word for "okra."

Serving Suggestion

Bake your favorite corn bread muffins, and serve them hot from the oven with plenty of creamy honey–butter. They're ideal companions to this spicy Creole specialty. Serve with a pitcher of cool and refreshing iced tea and slices of whipped cream–topped pecan pie for dessert.

3 tablespoons all-purpose flour

3 tablespoons vegetable oil

1/2 pound smoked pork sausage, cut into 1/2-inch slices

2 cups frozen cut okra

1 large onion, chopped (1 cup)

1 large green bell pepper, chopped (1 1/2 cups)

3 cloves garlic, finely chopped

1/4 teaspoon ground red pepper (cayenne)

1/4 teaspoon pepper

1 can (14 1/2 ounces) diced tomatoes, undrained

1 1/2 cups uncooked regular long-grain white rice

3 cups water

1 package (12 ounces) frozen cooked peeled and deveined medium shrimp, rinsed

1. Mix flour and oil in 1-quart heavy saucepan. Cook over medium-high heat 5 minutes, stirring constantly; reduce heat to medium. Cook about 10 minutes, stirring constantly, until mixture turns reddish brown.

2. Place flour-oil mixture in 3 1/2- to 4-quart slow cooker. Stir in remaining ingredients except rice, water and shrimp.

3. Cover and cook on low heat setting 7 to 9 hours or until okra is tender.

4. About 25 minutes before serving, cook rice in 3 cups water as directed on package. Meanwhile, stir shrimp into gumbo. Cover and cook on low heat setting 20 minutes. Serve gumbo over rice.

1 Serving: Calories 500 (Calories from Fat 180); Fat 20g (Saturated 5g); Cholesterol 140mg; Sodium 720mg; Carbohydrate 54g (Dietary Fiber 4g); Protein 26g • **% Daily Value:** Vitamin A 12%; Vitamin C 36%; Calcium 14%; Iron 28% • **Diet Exchanges:** 3 Starch, 2 Lean Meat, 2 Vegetable, 2 Fat • **Carbohydrate Choices:** 3 1/2

Pork Tortilla Soup

6 servings

SLOW COOKER:
3 1/2- to 4-quart

PREP TIME:
15 minutes

COOK TIME:
Low 6 to 8 hours

Ingredient Substitution

Great northern beans add a distinctive, delicate flavor to this Mexican-inspired soup, but you can substitute any canned beans you have on hand.

Serving Suggestion

Serve wedges of lime to squeeze a little fresh flavor into this hearty soup. Pass bowls of shredded Cheddar or Monterey Jack cheese, chopped fresh cilantro and sliced radishes to top each serving.

1 pound pork boneless sirloin or loin, cut into 1-inch cubes

1 envelope (1 1/4 ounces) taco seasoning mix

3 corn tortillas (5 or 6 inches in diameter), cut into 1-inch squares

1 can (14 1/2 ounces) diced tomatoes with jalapeños, undrained

2 cans (15 1/2 ounces each) great northern beans, drained

1 carton (32 ounces) chicken broth

4 corn tortillas (5 or 6 inches in diameter), cut in half, then cut into 1/2-inch strips

1. Mix all ingredients except tortilla strips in 3 1/2- to 4-quart slow cooker.

2. Cover and cook on low heat setting 6 to 8 hours or until pork is tender. Stir gently before serving. Place some tortilla strips into bottom of each of 6 bowls. Ladle soup over tortilla strips.

1 Serving: Calories 365 (Calories from Fat 45); Fat 5g (Saturated 1g); Cholesterol 40mg; Sodium 1180mg; Carbohydrate 56g (Dietary Fiber 11g); Protein 35g • **% Daily Value:** Vitamin A 14%; Vitamin C 8%; Calcium 20%; Iron 44% • **Diet Exchanges:** 3 1/2 Starch, 3 Very Lean Meat • **Carbohydrate Choices:** 4

Black-Eyed Pea and Sausage Soup

6 servings

SLOW COOKER:
3 1/2- to 4-quart

PREP TIME:
15 minutes

COOK TIME:
Low 8 to 9 hours

FINISHING COOK TIME:
Low 15 minutes

Ingredient Substitution

For those who enjoy other greens as well as spinach, use the greens solo or in combination with the spinach. Swiss chard, mustard greens and turnip greens are all good choices. Also, andouille sausage, a Cajun favorite, would give this soup even more of a kick.

Serving Suggestion

Black-eyed peas and sausage give this soup a southern flair. To spike it with even more flavor, offer Dijon mustard and prepared horseradish to stir in.

2 cans (15 to 16 ounces each) black-eyed peas, rinsed and drained

1 package (16 ounces) smoked turkey kielbasa sausage, cut lengthwise in half and then sliced

4 medium carrots, chopped (2 cups)

4 cloves garlic, finely chopped

1/2 cup uncooked wheat berries

1 cup water

3 cans (14 ounces each) beef broth

2 cups shredded fresh spinach

1 teaspoon dried marjoram leaves

1. Mix all ingredients except spinach and marjoram in 3 1/2- to 4-quart slow cooker.

2. Cover and cook on low heat setting 8 to 9 hours or until wheat berries are tender.

3. Stir in spinach and marjoram. Cover and cook on low heat setting about 15 minutes or until spinach is tender.

1 Serving: Calories 275 (Calories from Fat 70); Fat 8g (Saturated 2g); Cholesterol 40mg; Sodium 1400mg; Carbohydrate 37g (Dietary Fiber 11g); Protein 25g • **% Daily Value:** Vitamin A 100%; Vitamin C 6%; Calcium 8%; Iron 28% • **Diet Exchanges:** 2 Starch, 2 1/2 Very Lean Meat, 1 Vegetable • **Carbohydrate Choices:** 2 1/2

Smoky Ham and Navy Bean Stew

4 servings

SLOW COOKER:
3 1/2- to 4-quart

PREP TIME:
15 minutes

COOK TIME:
Low 10 to 12 hours

Betty's Success Tip

Liquid smoke is a liquid seasoning used to flavor meat, poultry and seafood. It is made by burning hickory chips and condensing the smoke into liquid form. A few drops go a long way, so use sparingly. Look for it in the barbecue and steak sauce section of your supermarket.

Serving Suggestion

A basket of warm baking powder biscuits served with spiced apple butter turns this stew into a simple, hearty meal. Fruit crisp topped with whipped cream provides the perfect ending to a nearly effortless dinner.

1 pound fully cooked smoked ham, cut into 1/2-inch cubes (3 cups)

1 cup dried navy beans, sorted and rinsed

2 medium stalks celery, sliced (1 cup)

1 small onion, chopped (1/4 cup)

2 medium carrots, sliced (1 cup)

2 cups water

1/4 teaspoon dried thyme leaves

1/4 teaspoon liquid smoke

1/4 cup chopped fresh parsley

1. Mix all ingredients except parsley in 3 1/2 to 4-quart slow cooker.

2. Cover and cook on low heat setting 10 to 12 hours or until beans are tender. Stir in parsley before serving.

1 Serving: Calories 360 (Calories from Fat 100); Fat 11g (Saturated 4g); Cholesterol 65mg; Sodium 1730mg; Carbohydrate 37g (Dietary Fiber 9g); Protein 37g • **% Daily Value:** Vitamin A 100%; Vitamin C 8%; Calcium 12%; Iron 28% • **Diet Exchanges:** 2 Starch, 4 Very Lean Meat, 1 Vegetable, 1 Fat • **Carbohydrate Choices:** 2 1/2

Chicken and Vegetable Tortellini Stew

6 servings

SLOW COOKER:
3 1/2- to 4-quart

PREP TIME:
35 minutes

COOK TIME:
Low 6 to 8 hours

FINISHING COOK TIME:
High 15 to 20 minutes

Ingredient Substitution

Save time cleaning and slicing carrots by using 1 cup baby-cut carrots. Keeping a bag of ready-to-eat baby-cut carrots on hand is helpful when it comes to making soups and stews.

Serving Suggestion

Serve with crusty garlic French bread and a salad of crisp Romaine lettuce, cherry tomatoes and thin slices of red onion tossed with your favorite Caesar or ranch dressing.

2 medium carrots, sliced (1 cup)

2 cloves garlic, finely chopped

1 pound boneless, skinless chicken thighs (5 thighs), cut into 3/4-inch pieces

1 medium fennel bulb, chopped

1 can (19 ounces) cannellini beans, rinsed and drained

1/2 teaspoon salt

1/4 teaspoon pepper

1 can (14 ounces) chicken broth

2 cups water

1 package (9 ounces) refrigerated cheese-filled tortellini

1 cup firmly packed fresh baby spinach leaves

2 medium green onions, sliced (2 tablespoons)

1 teaspoon dried basil leaves

2 tablespoons shredded fresh Parmesan cheese

1. Layer carrots, garlic, chicken, fennel and beans in 3 1/2- to 4-quart slow cooker. Sprinkle with salt and pepper. Pour broth and water over ingredients.

2. Cover and cook on low heat setting 6 to 8 hours or until chicken is no longer pink in center.

3. About 20 minutes before serving, stir tortellini, spinach, onions and basil into chicken mixture. Cover and cook on high heat setting 15 to 20 minutes or until tortellini are tender. Sprinkle individual servings with Parmesan cheese.

1 Serving: Calories 325 (Calories from Fat 100); Fat 11g (Saturated 4g); Cholesterol 85mg; Sodium 640mg; Carbohydrate 34g (Dietary Fiber 8g); Protein 31g • **% Daily Value:** Vitamin A 90%; Vitamin C 8%; Calcium 20%; Iron 32% • **Diet Exchanges:** 2 Starch, 3 1/2 Lean Meat • **Carbohydrate Choices:** 2

Chicken and Vegetable Tortellini Stew

Fisherman's Wharf Seafood Stew

6 servings

SLOW COOKER:
3 1/2- to 4-quart

PREP TIME:
35 minutes

COOK TIME:
Low 8 to 9 hours

FINISHING COOK TIME:
High 15 to 20 minutes

Betty's Success Tip

The easiest way to remove sand from a leek is to first cut the leek lengthwise, almost to the root end. Then, hold the leek under cool running water while fanning the leaves, so the water can wash out the sand.

Finishing Touch

For those who prefer fish stew with a little more spice, pass a bottle or two of your favorite hot green or red pepper sauce at the table.

2 tablespoons olive or vegetable oil

1 cup sliced leek (white and light green portion)

2 cloves garlic, finely chopped

1 cup sliced baby-cut carrots (1/4 inch thick)

3 cups sliced, quartered roma (plum) tomatoes (6 large)

1/2 cup chopped green bell pepper

1/2 teaspoon fennel seed

1 dried bay leaf

1 cup dry white wine or water

1 bottle (8 ounces) clam juice

1 pound cod (1 inch thick), cut into 1-inch pieces

1/2 pound uncooked peeled deveined medium shrimp

1 teaspoon sugar

1 teaspoon dried basil leaves

1/2 teaspoon salt

1/4 teaspoon red pepper sauce

2 tablespoons chopped fresh parsley

1. Mix oil, leek and garlic in 3 1/2- to 4-quart slow cooker. Add carrots, tomatoes, bell pepper, fennel seed, bay leaf, wine and clam juice; stir.

2. Cover and cook on low heat setting 8 to 9 hours or until vegetables are tender.

3. About 20 minutes before serving, gently stir in cod, shrimp, sugar, basil, salt and pepper sauce. Cover and cook on high heat setting 15 to 20 minutes or until fish flakes easily with fork. Remove bay leaf. Stir in parsley.

1 Serving: Calories 180 (Calories from Fat 55); Fat 6g (Saturated 1g); Cholesterol 95mg; Sodium 430mg; Carbohydrate 10g (Dietary Fiber 2g); Protein 22g • **% Daily Value:** Vitamin A 96%; Vitamin C 30%; Calcium 6%; Iron 12% • **Diet Exchanges:** 1/2 Starch, 2 1/2 Lean Meat, 1 Vegetable • **Carbohydrate Choices:** 1/2

Fisherman's Wharf Seafood Stew

Mexican Beef Stew

6 servings

SLOW COOKER:
3 1/2- to 4-quart

PREP TIME:
5 minutes

COOK TIME:
Low 9 to 11 hours

FINISHING COOK TIME:
High 15 to 30 minutes

Ingredient Substitution

Frozen small whole onions, also called pearl onions, are loaded with flavor and are so convenient to use. If you don't have them on hand, you can substitute 1/2 cup chopped onion.

Finishing Touch

Mexican-inspired dishes are fun to serve because everyone can personalize their serving. Pass shredded Mexican cheese blend, chopped avocado, sliced olives, sour cream and chopped fresh cilantro leaves for an extra-special touch.

2 pounds beef stew meat

1 can (28 ounces) whole tomatoes, undrained

1 cup frozen small whole onions (from 1-pound bag)

1 teaspoon chili powder

1 envelope (1 1/4 ounces) taco seasoning mix

1 can (15 ounces) black beans, rinsed and drained

1 can (11 ounces) whole kernel corn with red and green peppers, drained

1. Mix beef, tomatoes, frozen onions and chili powder in 3 1/2- to 4-quart slow cooker.

2. Cover and cook on low heat setting 9 to 11 hours or until beef is tender.

3. Stir in taco seasoning mix, using wire whisk. Stir in beans and corn. Cover and cook on high heat setting 15 to 30 minutes or until thickened.

1 Serving: Calories 440 (Calories from Fat 160); Fat 18g (Saturated 7g); Cholesterol 95mg; Sodium 850mg; Carbohydrate 38g (Dietary Fiber 8g); Protein 40g • **% Daily Value:** Vitamin A 24%; Vitamin C 20%; Calcium 10%; Iron 34% • **Diet Exchanges:** 2 1/2 Starch, 4 1/2 Lean Meat • **Carbohydrate Choices:** 2 1/2

Mexican Beef Stew

Scottish Lamb Stew

6 servings

SLOW COOKER:
3 1/2- to 4-quart

PREP TIME:
20 minutes

COOK TIME:
Low 9 to 10 hours

FINISHING COOK TIME:
Low 15 minutes

Ingredient Substitution

Beef stew meat can be used instead of the lamb. For a heartier taste with a subtle nutty flavor, use 1 cup of ale or dark beer in place of 1 cup of the chicken broth.

Serving Suggestion

Quick-cooking barley cooks up fast and can be made when the peas are stirred into the stew. Common in Scottish cooking, barley complements this lamb stew nicely.

1/3 cup all-purpose flour

1/2 teaspoon ground mustard

1/2 teaspoon seasoned salt

2 pounds lamb boneless shoulder or stew meat, cut into 1 1/2-inch pieces

1 tablespoon vegetable oil

3 medium potatoes, cut into 1-inch pieces

2 medium carrots, cut into 1/2-inch pieces

1 cup frozen small whole onions (from 1-pound bag)

1 teaspoon seasoned salt

2 1/4 cups chicken broth

1 1/2 cups frozen green peas (from 1-pound bag)

Hot cooked barley or rice, if desired

Apple mint jelly, if desired

1. Place flour, mustard and 1/2 teaspoon seasoned salt in resealable plastic food-storage bag. Add lamb; toss to coat. Heat oil in 12-inch skillet over medium-high heat. Cook lamb in oil, stirring occasionally, until brown.

2. Place potatoes, carrots and onions in 3 1/2- to 4-quart slow cooker. Sprinkle with 1 teaspoon seasoned salt. Place lamb on vegetables. Pour broth over lamb.

3. Cover and cook on low heat setting 9 to 10 hours or until lamb is tender.

4. Stir in peas. Cover and cook on low heat setting 15 minutes. Serve stew with barley and jelly.

1 Serving: Calories 385 (Calories from Fat 125); Fat 14g (Saturated 4g); Cholesterol 110mg; Sodium 850mg; Carbohydrate 26g (Dietary Fiber 4g); Protein 39g • **% Daily Value:** Vitamin A 78%; Vitamin C 8%; Calcium 4%; Iron 22% • **Diet Exchanges:** 1 1/2 Starch, 4 1/2 Lean Meat, 1 Vegetable • **Carbohydrate Choices:** 2

Scottish Lamb Stew

Curried Pork Stew

6 servings

SLOW COOKER:
3 1/2- to 4-quart

PREP TIME:
20 minutes

COOK TIME:
Low 8 to 9 hours

FINISHING COOK TIME:
Low 1 hour

Betty's Success Tip

Curry powder is a blend that can be made with up to twenty different spices. Therefore, it can vary in taste from blend to blend. To get the best flavor, use your favorite curry powder.

Serving Suggestion

Serve this stew over basmati rice along with yogurt, mango chutney, cilantro and pita folds or Indian naan bread.

3 tablespoons all-purpose flour

2 tablespoons curry powder

1/2 teaspoon salt

1 pound pork boneless center cut loin, cut into 1-inch pieces

1 tablespoon olive or vegetable oil

1 medium onion, chopped (1/2 cup)

1 pound small red potatoes, cut into fourths (3 cups)

1 can (14 1/2 ounces) whole tomatoes, undrained

1/2 cup apple juice

2 1/2 cups cauliflowerets

1. Mix flour, 1 tablespoon of the curry powder and the salt in resealable plastic food-storage bag. Add pork; toss to coat. Heat oil in 10-inch skillet over medium-high heat. Cook pork in oil, stirring occasionally, until brown.

2. Place onion and potatoes in 3 1/2- to 4-quart slow cooker. Top with pork and tomatoes. Mix apple juice and remaining 1 tablespoon curry powder; pour over pork.

3. Cover and cook on low heat setting 8 to 9 hours or until pork and potatoes are tender.

4. Stir in cauliflowerets. Cover and cook on low heat setting about 1 hour or until cauliflower is tender.

1 Serving: Calories 360 (Calories from Fat 110); Fat 12g (Saturated 4g); Cholesterol 70mg; Sodium 420mg; Carbohydrate 38g (Dietary Fiber 5g); Protein 30g • **% Daily Value:** Vitamin A 6%; Vitamin C 46%; Calcium 6%; Iron 20% • **Diet Exchanges:** 1 Starch, 2 Medium-Fat Meat, 5 Vegetable • **Carbohydrate Choices:** 2 1/2

Curried Pork Stew

Vegetable Beef Stew

4 servings

SLOW COOKER:
3 1/2- to 4-quart

PREP TIME:
10 minutes

COOK TIME:
Low 8 to 10 hours

Betty's Success Tip

It saves time to use stew beef, but take a few minutes to trim any extra fat off the beef before adding it to the bag with the stew seasoning. This will help reduce the amount of fat in the finished dish.

Finishing Touch

Ladle the stew into bowls, and sprinkle each serving with crumbled crisply cooked bacon and chopped fresh parsley. Serve with chunks of warm crusty bread to soak up all the flavorful gravy.

1 1/2 cups baby-cut carrots

2 medium potatoes, peeled and cut into 1-inch pieces

1 medium stalk celery, cut into 1-inch pieces

1 envelope (1 1/2 ounces) beef stew seasoning

1 pound beef stew meat

1 cup water

1 cup frozen whole kernel corn (from 1-pound bag)

1 cup frozen cut green beans (from 1-pound bag)

1. Layer carrots, potatoes and celery in 3 1/2- to 4-quart slow cooker. Place stew seasoning in resealable plastic food-storage bag. Add beef; toss to coat. Add beef to cooker; sprinkle with any remaining seasoning. Pour in water. Layer frozen corn and green beans on top.

2. Cover and cook on low heat setting 8 to 10 hours until beef is tender. Stir stew before serving.

1 Serving: Calories 330 (Calories from Fat 115); Fat 13g (Saturated 5g); Cholesterol 70mg; Sodium 680mg; Carbohydrate 28g (Dietary Fiber 5g); Protein 26g • **% Daily Value:** Vitamin A 100%; Vitamin C 10%; Calcium 4%; Iron 18% • **Diet Exchanges:** 1 1/2 Starch, 3 Lean Meat, 1 Vegetable, 1/2 Fat • **Carbohydrate Choices:** 2

White Chili with Chicken

6 servings

SLOW COOKER:
3 1/2- to 4-quart

PREP TIME:
15 minutes

COOK TIME:
Low 8 to 10 hours

Betty's Success Tip

White chili—usually made with white beans, chicken and chilies instead of red beans, beef and tomatoes—is still packed with plenty of spicy chili flavor. You can add more kick by increasing the amount of red pepper sauce.

Ingredient Substitution

Keep a package of frozen diced cooked chicken in the freezer. It's a lifesaver when you're in a big hurry and don't have time to cut chicken into strips.

1 pound boneless, skinless chicken thighs (5 thighs), cut into thin strips

1 cup dried great northern beans, sorted and rinsed

1 medium onion, chopped (1/2 cup)

1 clove garlic, finely chopped

2 teaspoons dried oregano leaves

1/2 teaspoon salt

1 can (10 3/4 ounces) condensed cream of chicken soup

5 cups water

1 teaspoon ground cumin

1/4 teaspoon red pepper sauce

1 can (4 1/2 ounces) chopped green chiles, undrained

1. Mix chicken, beans, onion, garlic, oregano, salt, soup and water in 3 1/2- to 4-quart slow cooker.

2. Cover and cook on low heat setting 8 to 10 hours or until beans are tender and chicken is no longer pink in center.

3. Just before serving, stir in cumin, pepper sauce and chiles. Serve with additional red pepper sauce if desired.

1 Serving: Calories 260 (Calories from Fat 80); Fat 9g (Saturated 3g); Cholesterol 50mg; Sodium 700mg; Carbohydrate 23g (Dietary Fiber 6g); Protein 21g • **% Daily Value:** Vitamin A 6%; Vitamin C 10%; Calcium 10%; Iron 20% • **Diet Exchanges:** 1 1/2 Starch, 2 1/2 Lean Meat • **Carbohydrate Choices:** 1 1/2

Chunky Chicken Chili with Hominy

6 servings

SLOW COOKER:
3 1/2- to 4-quart

PREP TIME:
5 minutes

COOK TIME:
Low 7 to 9 hours

FINISHING COOK TIME:
Low 15 minutes

Betty's Success Tip

Go ahead and make the chili ahead of time and refrigerate or freeze. Chili is often better the next day because the flavors have a chance to blend. Thaw frozen chili in the refrigerator, and reheat in a saucepan over medium-low heat, stirring occasionally, until hot.

Ingredient Substitution

For extra spice, use hot chili seasoning instead of the mild, and add a small can of chopped green chiles with the tomatoes. You can also vary the taste by using black beans or chili beans instead of the hominy.

2 pounds boneless, skinless chicken thighs (10 thighs)

2 cans (14 1/2 ounces each) diced tomatoes with green chilies, undrained

1 can (15 ounces) tomato sauce

1 envelope (1 1/4 ounces) mild chili seasoning mix

2 cans (15 1/2 ounces each) hominy or posole, drained

Sour cream, if desired

Cilantro, if desired

1. Place chicken in 3 1/2- to 4-quart slow cooker. Mix tomatoes, tomato sauce and chili seasoning; pour over chicken.

2. Cover and cook on low heat setting 7 to 9 hours or until chicken is no longer pink in center.

3. Stir to break up chicken. Stir in hominy. Cover and cook on low heat setting about 15 minutes until heated through. Serve chili with sour cream and cilantro.

1 Serving: Calories 365 (Calories from Fat 125); Fat 14g (Saturated 4g); Cholesterol 95mg; Sodium 1640mg; Carbohydrate 31g (Dietary Fiber 7g); Protein 36g • **% Daily Value:** Vitamin A 34%; Vitamin C 30%; Calcium 12%; Iron 26% • **Diet Exchanges:** 2 Starch, 4 Lean Meat • **Carbohydrate Choices:** 2

Mexican Beef Chili

6 servings

SLOW COOKER:
3 1/2- to 4-quart

PREP TIME:
15 minutes

COOK TIME:
Low 8 to 10 hours

Betty's Success Tip

Cinnamon sticks and baking cocoa may seem like odd ingredients for a chili recipe, but the two ingredients are based on the spicy Mexican mole sauce that includes Mexican or bitter chocolate. Baking cocoa makes the sauce taste richer without adding sweetness.

Finishing Touch

This chili is flavorful and delicious on its own. But a dollop of sour cream, a sprinkle of sliced green onions and shredded Cheddar cheese make it extra special.

2 pounds beef boneless chuck, cut into 1-inch cubes

2 tablespoons chili powder

1/2 teaspoon salt

1 teaspoon ground cumin

2 tablespoons instant chopped onion

1/2 teaspoon garlic powder

1 can (15 1/2 ounces) dark red kidney beans, drained

2 cans (14 1/2 ounces each) diced tomatoes with basil, garlic and oregano, undrained

1 tablespoon baking cocoa

2 cinnamon sticks

1. Mix all ingredients in 3 1/2- to 4-quart slow cooker.

2. Cover and cook on low heat setting 8 to 10 hours or until beef is tender. Remove cinnamon sticks before serving.

1 Serving: Calories 395 (Calories from Fat 160); Fat 18g (Saturated 7g); Cholesterol 95mg; Sodium 670mg; Carbohydrate 26g (Dietary Fiber 7g); Protein 39g • **% Daily Value:** Vitamin A 28%; Vitamin C 18%; Calcium 8%; Iron 38% • **Diet Exchanges:** 2 Starch, 4 Lean Meat • **Carbohydrate Choices:** 2

Spicy Black Bean Barbecue Chili

6 servings

SLOW COOKER:
3 1/2- to 4-quart

PREP TIME:
15 minutes

STAND TIME:
1 hour

COOK TIME:
Low 10 to 12 hours

FINISHING COOK TIME:
High 30 minutes

Betty's Success Tip

Get a jump start on making this spicy chili by soaking the beans in cold water overnight rather than using the quick-soak method.

Finishing Touch

Black beans and rice are a natural pair. Serve this hearty vegetarian chili over a mound of cooked rice and top with chopped bell pepper and fresh cilantro for added color and flavor.

2 cups dried black beans, sorted and rinsed

10 cups water

1 tablespoon olive or vegetable oil

1 large onion, chopped (1 cup)

6 cloves garlic, finely chopped

4 cups water

1 can (14 1/2 ounces) diced tomatoes with green chilies, undrained

1 cup hickory barbecue sauce

1 chipotle chili in adobo sauce, finely chopped, plus 1 teaspoon adobo sauce (from 7-ounce can)

2 cups frozen veggie crumbles

1. Heat beans and 10 cups water to boiling in 4-quart Dutch oven; reduce heat. Simmer uncovered 10 minutes; remove from heat. Cover and let stand 1 hour.

2. Heat oil in 10-inch skillet over medium-high heat. Cook onion and garlic in oil about 8 minutes, stirring occasionally, until onion is tender and light golden brown.

3. Drain beans. Place beans in 3 1/2- to 4-quart slow cooker. Add 4 cups water and onion mixture.

4. Cover and cook on low heat setting 10 to 12 hours or until beans are tender.

5. Stir in tomatoes, barbecue sauce, chili, adobo sauce and frozen veggie crumbles. Cover and cook on high heat setting 30 minutes.

1 Serving: Calories 350 (Calories from Fat 35); Fat 4g (Saturated 1g); Cholesterol 0mg; Sodium 840mg; Carbohydrate 66g (Dietary Fiber 11g); Protein 22g • **% Daily Value:** Vitamin A 10%; Vitamin C 30%; Calcium 16%; Iron 34% • **Diet Exchanges:** 4 Starch, 1 Very Lean Meat, 1 Vegetable • **Carbohydrate Choices:** 4 1/2

BettyCrocker.com

Spicy Black Bean Barbecue Chili

3

Easiest-Ever
Main Meals

- Chicken Stew 68
- Chicken–Wild Rice Casserole with Dried Cherries 69
- Turkey Breast with Sherried Stuffing 70
- Turkey Verde 72
- Turkey Sausage–Bean Bake 74
- Harvest Sausage-Vegetable Casserole 75
- Beef Carbonnade with Potatoes 76
- Beef Pot Roast with Vegetables 78
- Corned Beef Brisket with Horseradish Sour Cream 79
- Zesty Italian Beef Tips 80
- Country-Style Ribs and Sauerkraut 81
- Asian Hoisin Ribs 82
- Apricot-Glazed Pork Roast and Stuffing 84
- Green Chile and Pork Stew 86
- Ham with Fruit Chutney 87
- Ham with Cheesy Potatoes 88
- Ham and Lentil Stew 90

◄ Chicken Stew (page 68)

Chicken Stew

6 servings

Photo on page 66

SLOW COOKER:
3 1/2- to 4-quart

PREP TIME:
12 minutes

COOK TIME:
Low 8 to 10 hours

Betty's Success Tip

A variety of fresh mushrooms work well in this satisfying stew. Try crimini, shiitake or white or brown button mushrooms. Use one kind, or mix two or three different types of mushroom together.

Serving Suggestion

Serve the stew in individual pasta bowls with chunks of crusty bread to soak up every last drop of sauce leftover in the dish. If you like peas in your stew, heat 1 cup of frozen green peas in the microwave and stir into the stew before serving.

3 medium potatoes (about 1 pound), cut into 1 1/2-inch cubes

2 cups baby-cut carrots

1 package (8 ounces) fresh whole mushrooms, cut in half

12 boneless, skinless chicken thighs (about 2 1/2 pounds)

1/2 teaspoon salt

1 teaspoon instant chopped onion

1/4 teaspoon garlic powder

1 tablespoon tomato paste

1 jar (15 ounces) roasted chicken gravy

1/2 cup dry white wine or water

1. Toss potatoes, carrots and mushrooms in 3 1/2- to 4-quart slow cooker. Arrange chicken on top. Sprinkle salt, onion and garlic powder over chicken. Stir tomato paste into jar of gravy. Pour gravy mixture and wine over all.

2. Cover and cook on low heat setting 8 to 10 hours or until vegetables are tender.

1 Serving: Calories 365 (Calories from Fat 135); Fat 15g (Saturated 5g); Cholesterol 85mg; Sodium 740mg; Carbohydrate 25g (Dietary Fiber 3g); Protein 35g • **% Daily Value:** Vitamin A 100%; Vitamin C 10%; Calcium 6%; Iron 22% • **Diet Exchanges:** 1 1/2 Starch, 4 Lean Meat • **Carbohydrate Choices:** 1 1/2

Chicken–Wild Rice Casserole with Dried Cherries

8 servings

SLOW COOKER:
6-quart

PREP TIME:
18 minutes

COOK TIME:
High 4 to 6 hours

Betty's Success Tip

It's worth taking a few extra minutes to remove the skin from the drumsticks and thighs. The skin doesn't brown during cooking, so it won't enhance the appearance of the dish.

Finishing Touch

This casserole is a great recipe to make for the holidays. The chunky applesauce and dried cherries or cranberries add a sweet and tart flavor. Parmesan cheese and toasted almonds are a natural with wild rice and chicken. Sprinkle a bit of both over the top of this comfort-food casserole.

1 1/2 cups uncooked wild rice

1/3 cup dried cherries or cranberries

1 tablespoon instant chopped onion

1 cup baby-cut carrots

2 medium stalks celery, cut into 2-inch pieces (1 cup)

1 cup chunky applesauce

1/2 teaspoon salt

8 chicken drumsticks, skin removed (about 2 pounds)

8 chicken thighs, skin removed (about 2 pounds)

1 can (10 3/4 ounces) condensed beefy mushroom soup

1 can (14 ounces) chicken broth

2 teaspoons dried thyme leaves

1. Mix wild rice, cherries, onion, carrots, celery, applesauce and salt in 6-quart slow cooker. Arrange chicken drumsticks and thighs over rice mixture. Pour soup over chicken; pour broth over all. Sprinkle thyme on chicken.

2. Cover and cook on high heat setting 4 to 6 hours or until wild rice is tender.

1 Serving: Calories 390 (Calories from Fat 80); Fat 9g (Saturated 3g); Cholesterol 95mg; Sodium 710mg; Carbohydrate 42g (Dietary Fiber 4g); Protein 35g • **% Daily Value:** Vitamin A 82%; Vitamin C 4%; Calcium 4%; Iron 20% • **Diet Exchanges:** 3 Starch, 3 1/2 Very Lean Meat, 1/2 Fat • **Carbohydrate Choices:** 3

Turkey Breast with Sherried Stuffing

6 servings

SLOW COOKER:
3 1/2- to 4-quart

PREP TIME:
20 minutes

COOK TIME:
Low 6 to 7 hours

STAND TIME:
10 minutes

Ingredient Substitution

No sherry on hand? Use apple juice, apple cider or chicken broth instead to keep the stuffing moist and flavorful.

Serving Suggestion

Use any leftover turkey to make sandwiches the next day. Place the sliced turkey (cold or reheated) between slices of whole-grain bread. Reheat the leftover stuffing in the microwave and add a big spoonful of stuffing next to each sandwich. Warm a jar of roasted turkey gravy in the microwave and pour over the sandwiches. What could be easier!

1/4 cup chopped onion

1 medium stalk celery, sliced (1/2 cup)

2- to 2 1/2-pound boneless, skinless turkey breast half, thawed if frozen

1 jar (12 ounces) roasted turkey gravy

1/3 cup dry sherry

1 package (6 ounces) turkey-flavor one-step stuffing mix

1. Spray 3 1/2- to 4-quart slow cooker with cooking spray. Place onion and celery in cooker. Top with turkey breast half. Pour gravy and sherry over top. Top with dry stuffing.

2. Cover and cook on low heat setting 6 to 7 hours or until turkey is no longer pink when center is cut.

3. About 15 minutes before serving, remove turkey from cooker; place on cutting board. Stir stuffing and cooking juices until mixed. Cover and let stand 10 minutes. Cut turkey into slices; serve with stuffing.

1 Serving: Calories 320 (Calories from Fat 55); Fat 6g (Saturated 1g); Cholesterol 100mg; Sodium 870mg; Carbohydrate 27g (Dietary Fiber 1g); Protein 40g • **% Daily Value:** Vitamin A 8%; Vitamin C 0%; Calcium 6%; Iron 18% • **Diet Exchanges:** 2 Starch, 5 Very Lean Meat, 1/2 Fat • **Carbohydrate Choices:** 2

Simple Sides and Desserts

Many dishes prepared in a slow cooker are meals in and of themselves. But variety, as the saying goes, is the spice of life, so it never hurts to offer a simple salad or side dish to make a slow cooker meal more complete. Not sure where to start? Here are some ideas to help make your dinner well rounded.

Simple Salads

Peach and Plum Salad

Divide 3 sliced peaches and 3 sliced plums among 6 serving plates. Sprinkle with 1/2 cup chopped walnuts. Drizzle with raspberry vinaigrette.

Honey-Lime Fruit Salad

Mix 1/2 cup honey, 1/2 cup frozen (thawed) limeade concentrate and 1 tablespoon poppy seed in large bowl. Add 12 cups cut-up fresh fruit (cantaloupe, kiwifruit, pink grapefruit) to honey mixture; carefully toss. Sprinkle with toasted slivered almonds.

Black Bean and Corn Salad

Mix 1 can (15 ounces) black beans, rinsed and drained; 1 can (about 8 ounces) whole kernel corn, drained; 1 can (4 ounces) chopped green chilies, drained; 1/2 cup medium salsa; 1/4 cup chopped onion; and 2 tablespoons chopped fresh cilantro in large bowl. Cover and refrigerate 15 minutes.

Satisfying Sides

Pesto Vegetables

Cook and drain a 1-pound bag of frozen vegetables (such as broccoli, cauliflower and carrots) as directed on package. Toss vegetables with 1/3 cup basil pesto. Sprinkle with 1 tablespoon grated Parmesan cheese.

Caesar Vegetable Medley

Heat 2 tablespoons olive oil in 10-inch nonstick skillet over medium-high heat. Add two 1-pound bags of frozen vegetables (such as cauliflower, carrots and snow pea pods) and 1 envelope (1.2 ounces) Caesar salad dressing mix. Cover and cook 5 to 7 minutes, stirring frequently, until vegetables are crisp-tender.

Asparagus with Mustard

Cover and cook 12 to 16 asparagus spears in boiling water until crisp-tender, about 8 minutes; drain. Shake 3 tablespoons honey, 2 tablespoons Dijon mustard, 4 teaspoons lemon juice and 2 teaspoons olive oil in tightly covered container; drizzle over asparagus.

Delectable Desserts

Honey-Chocolate Sundaes

Mix 1/2 cup honey and 1/4 cup apricot brandy or apricot nectar. Spoon over chocolate ice cream in each of 4 dessert dishes. Sprinkle each dish with about 1/2 teaspoon baking cocoa.

Brown Sugar Strawberries

Place 2 pints (4 cups) unhulled strawberries in serving bowl. Place 2/3 cup each plain yogurt and brown sugar in separate bowls. Dip strawberries in yogurt, then into brown sugar.

Rice and Raisin Pudding

Heat 1 cup uncooked instant rice, 1 cup milk, 1/4 cup raisins, 3 tablespoons sugar, 1/4 teaspoon each salt and ground cinnamon to boiling in saucepan, stirring constantly; remove from heat. Cover, let stand 5 minutes.

Turkey Verde

6 servings

SLOW COOKER:
3 1/2- to 4-quart

PREP TIME:
15 minutes

COOK TIME:
Low 8 to 10 hours

Betty's Success Tip

To warm tortillas before serving, wrap them in aluminum foil and heat in a 325° oven for about 15 minutes. Or place on a microwavable paper towel and microwave on High for 30 seconds.

Ingredient Substitution

Verde means "green" in Spanish, so Turkey Verde simply means turkey in green sauce. Green sauce also complements pork, so try this with a 2 1/2-pound pork boneless loin roast in place of the turkey breast.

2 1/2-pound boneless turkey breast half, thawed if frozen and skin removed

1 jar (16 ounces) mild green salsa

1 medium onion, chopped (1/2 cup)

1 medium potato, chopped (3/4 cup)

4 cloves garlic, finely chopped

1/2 cup chicken broth

1 teaspoon ground cumin

6 flour tortillas (8 to 10 inches in diameter), warmed

1. Place turkey in 3 1/2- to 4-quart slow cooker. Mix salsa, onion, potato, garlic, broth and cumin; pour over turkey.

2. Cover and cook on low heat setting 8 to 10 hours or until turkey is no longer pink when center is cut.

3. Remove turkey from cooker; place on cutting board. Cut turkey into slices; serve with sauce and tortillas.

1 Serving: Calories 375 (Calories from Fat 45); Fat 5g (Saturated 1g); Cholesterol 125mg; Sodium 700mg; Carbohydrate 35g (Dietary Fiber 3g); Protein 50g • **% Daily Value:** Vitamin A 10%; Vitamin C 10%; Calcium 10%; Iron 26% • **Diet Exchanges:** 2 Starch, 6 Very Lean Meat, 1 Vegetable • **Carbohydrate Choices:** 2

Turkey Verde

Turkey Sausage–Bean Bake

4 servings

SLOW COOKER:
2- to 3 1/2-quart

PREP TIME:
20 minutes

COOK TIME:
Low 6 to 8 hours

Betty's Success Tip

Dried leaf herbs are called for in most slow cooker recipes because they tend to hold their flavor better than fresh herbs during long cooking times. However, if you have fresh herbs on hand, stir in 1 tablespoon fresh marjoram and 1 teaspoon fresh thyme leaves at the end of the cooking time.

Ingredient Substitution

It doesn't matter what type of beans you use in this recipe. Butter, kidney and black beans are super alternatives to the great northern beans.

1/2 pound fully cooked smoked turkey sausage ring, cut into 1/2-inch slices

2/3 cup shredded carrot

1/4 cup chopped onion

2 cans (15 1/2 ounces each) great northern beans, drained and 3/4 cup liquid reserved

1 teaspoon dried marjoram leaves

1/4 teaspoon dried thyme leaves

1/4 teaspoon pepper

1. Mix all ingredients including reserved bean liquid in 2- to 3 1/2-quart slow cooker.

2. Cover and cook on low heat setting 6 to 8 hours, or until hot and bubbly, to blend and develop flavors.

1 Serving: Calories 335 (Calories from Fat 55); Fat 6g (Saturated 2g); Cholesterol 30mg; Sodium 580mg; Carbohydrate 55g (Dietary Fiber 14g); Protein 29g • **% Daily Value:** Vitamin A 68%; Vitamin C 2%; Calcium 20%; Iron 45% • **Diet Exchanges:** 3 1/2 Starch, 2 Very Lean Meat • **Carbohydrate Choices:** 3 1/2

Harvest Sausage-Vegetable Casserole

4 servings

SLOW COOKER:
3 1/2- to 4-quart

PREP TIME:
20 minutes

COOK TIME:
Low 7 to 8 hours

Ingredient Substitution

Diced tomatoes come in a variety of flavors such as roasted garlic, crushed red pepper and basil and olive oil, garlic and spices. Feel free to use your favorite in this tasty casserole.

Serving Suggestion

Freshly baked baking powder biscuits are a nice addition to this full-flavored dish. Pass the Dijon mustard for those who want to add a dollop to their stew.

3 tablespoons zesty Italian dressing

1 tablespoon Dijon mustard

2 medium unpeeled potatoes, cut into 1/2-inch slices (2 cups)

2 medium onions, sliced (1 1/2 cups)

2 medium carrots, cut into 1/2-inch slices (1 cup)

2 cups chopped green cabbage

1 ring (1 pound) fully cooked smoked turkey or chicken sausage, cut into 1/2-inch slices

1 can (14 1/2 ounces) diced tomatoes with green pepper, celery and onion, undrained

1. Mix dressing and mustard. Arrange potato slices in even layer in 3 1/2- to 4-quart slow cooker; drizzle with one-third of the dressing mixture. Arrange onion slices on potatoes; drizzle with one-third of the dressing mixture. Top with carrots and cabbage; drizzle with remaining dressing mixture.

2. Arrange sausage slices on vegetables. Pour tomatoes in even layer over sausage.

3. Cover and cook on low heat setting 7 to 8 hours or until vegetables are tender.

1 Serving: Calories 335 (Calories from Fat 135); Fat 15g (Saturated 3g); Cholesterol 60mg; Sodium 1630mg; Carbohydrate 34g (Dietary Fiber 5g); Protein 21g • **% Daily Value:** Vitamin A 100%; Vitamin C 32%; Calcium 10%; Iron 14% • **Diet Exchanges:** 2 Starch, 2 Medium-Fat Meat, 1 Vegetable •
Carbohydrate Choices: 1 1/2

Beef Carbonnade with Potatoes

8 servings

SLOW COOKER:
3 1/2- to 4-quart

PREP TIME:
12 minutes

COOK TIME:
Low 8 to 10 hours

Betty's Success Tip

Carbonnade is a French term that describes any meat cooked over hot coals or directly over flames. We simplified the process by converting the dish into a slow cooker recipe.

Ingredient Substitution

If you prefer to skip the beer, use the same quantity of non-alcoholic beer, apple cider or beef broth instead. And if you can't find tomato beef oxtail soup mix at your supermarket, use a 10 3/4-ounce can of condensed tomato soup with 1 teaspoon beef bouillon granules instead.

1 medium onion, sliced

8 small red potatoes, cut into fourths

2 1/2-pound beef round steak, cut into 8 serving pieces

1 tablespoon packed brown sugar

1/2 teaspoon ground nutmeg

1/2 teaspoon salt

1/4 teaspoon pepper

1 package (1.8 ounces) tomato beef flavor (oxtail) soup mix

1 can (12 ounces) beer

1. Place onion and potatoes in 3 1/2- to 4-quart slow cooker. Arrange beef on top. Sprinkle beef with brown sugar, nutmeg, salt, pepper and soup mix (dry). Pour beer over all.

2. Cover and cook on low heat setting 8 to 10 hours or until beef is tender.

3. Spoon pan juices over beef before serving.

1 Serving: Calories 310 (Calories from Fat 45); Fat 5g (Saturated 2g); Cholesterol 75mg; Sodium 600mg; Carbohydrate 35g (Dietary Fiber 3g); Protein 31g • **% Daily Value:** Vitamin A 4%; Vitamin C 14%; Calcium 3%; Iron 22% • **Diet Exchanges:** 2 Starch, 3 Very Lean Meat, 1 Vegetable • **Carbohydrate Choices:** 2

Beef Carbonnade with Potatoes

Beef Pot Roast with Vegetables

6 servings

SLOW COOKER:
3 1/2- to 4-quart

PREP TIME:
12 minutes

COOK TIME:
Low 9 to 10 hours

Betty's Success Tip

Because the grain in a pot roast changes direction, it isn't always easy to get tender slices. To slice pot roast, place the roast on a carving board or platter. Hold the meat in place with a meat fork, and cut between the muscles. Remove one section of the meat at a time. Turn the section so that the grain of the meat runs parallel to the carving board, and cut meat across the grain into 1/4-inch slices.

Ingredient Substitution

If you've used the last of your chili sauce, not to worry; ketchup will do in a pinch.

3-pound beef boneless chuck pot roast

2 dried bay leaves

2 medium stalks celery, cut into 3-inch pieces

6 small red potatoes, cut into fourths

1 cup baby-cut carrots

1 jar (4.5 ounces) whole mushrooms, drained

1 can (10 3/4 ounces) condensed cream of mushroom soup

2 tablespoons chili sauce

1/2 package (2.2-ounce size) beefy onion soup mix (1 envelope)

1. Place beef in 3 1/2- to 4-quart slow cooker. Arrange bay leaves on top of beef; arrange celery, potatoes, carrots and mushrooms around beef. Top beef with condensed mushroom soup, chili sauce and beefy onion soup mix (dry).

2. Cover and cook on low heat setting 9 to 10 hours or until beef is tender. Discard bay leaves.

1 Serving: Calories 595 (Calories from Fat 260); Fat 29g (Saturated 11g); Cholesterol 140mg; Sodium 1100mg; Carbohydrate 34g (Dietary Fiber 4g); Protein 50g • **% Daily Value:** Vitamin A 80%; Vitamin C 14%; Calcium 6%; Iron 38% • **Diet Exchanges:** 2 Starch, 6 Lean Meat, 1 Vegetable, 2 Fat • **Carbohydrate Choices:** 2

Corned Beef Brisket
with Horseradish Sour Cream

8 servings

SLOW COOKER:
5- to 6-quart

PREP TIME:
10 minutes

COOK TIME:
Low 8 to 9 hours

Betty's Success Tip

Corned beef was originally "corned," or preserved with granular salt, because there was no refrigeration. Today, the beef is cured in brine and spices are added for a distinctive tangy flavor. Because we use crushed red pepper flakes in this recipe, there's no need to use the additional seasonings found in the seasoning packet.

Serving Suggestion

Boiled potatoes and cabbage complement the spicy flavor of corned beef. Serve this corned beef brisket with boiled small red potatoes and steamed green cabbage wedges and add slices of hearty rye bread to round out the meal.

1 large sweet onion (Bermuda, Maui, Spanish, Walla Walla), sliced

3- to 3 1/2-pound well-trimmed corned beef brisket

3/4 teaspoon crushed red pepper flakes

1 cup reduced-sodium chicken broth

1 tablespoon Worcestershire sauce

Horseradish Sour Cream (below)

1. Place onion in 5- to 6-quart slow cooker. Thoroughly rinse beef; discard seasoning packet. Place beef on onion; sprinkle with red pepper. Mix broth and Worcestershire sauce; pour over beef.

2. Cover and cook on low heat setting 8 to 9 hours or until beef is tender.

3. Remove beef from cooker; place on cutting board. Remove onion with slotted spoon; cover with aluminum foil to keep warm. Cut beef against grain into slices. Serve with onion and Horseradish Sour Cream.

Horseradish Sour Cream

1/2 cup sour cream

1 tablespoon cream-style horseradish

2 tablespoons chopped fresh parsley

Mix all ingredients.

1 Serving: Calories 340 (Calories from Fat 235); Fat 26g (Saturated 9g); Cholesterol 130mg; Sodium 1460mg; Carbohydrate 3g (Dietary Fiber 0g); Protein 23g • **% Daily Value:** Vitamin A 6%; Vitamin C 2%; Calcium 2%; Iron 14% • **Diet Exchanges:** 3 1/2 High-Fat Meat • **Carbohydrate Choices:** 0

Zesty Italian Beef Tips

6 servings

SLOW COOKER:
3 1/2- to 4-quart

PREP TIME:
10 minutes

COOK TIME:
Low 8 to 10 hours

2 pounds beef stew meat

1 cup frozen small whole onions (from 1-pound bag)

1 jar (6 ounces) pitted Kalamata or Greek olives, drained

1/3 cup sun-dried tomatoes in oil, drained and chopped

1 jar (28 ounces) marinara sauce

6 cups hot cooked pasta

1. Place beef and frozen onions in 3 1/2- to 4-quart slow cooker. Top with olives and tomatoes. Pour marinara sauce over top.

2. Cover and cook on low heat setting 8 to 10 hours or until beef is tender. Serve over pasta.

Betty's Success Tip

If the beef stew meat comes in different size chunks, cut up the larger pieces so all are the same size. This ensures even cooking so every bite will be tender.

Ingredient Substitution

Kalamata or Greek olives can be found in jars or in olive bars at the supermarket. They add a pleasant, tangy flavor to this dish, but large ripe olives can be substituted if desired.

1 Serving: Calories 660 (Calories from Fat 245); Fat 27g (Saturated 8g); Cholesterol 95mg; Sodium 990mg; Carbohydrate 69g (Dietary Fiber 5g); Protein 40g • **% Daily Value:** Vitamin A 22%; Vitamin C 22%; Calcium 8%; Iron 40% • **Diet Exchanges:** 4 Starch, 3 1/2 Medium-Fat Meat, 2 Vegetable, 1 Fat • **Carbohydrate Choices:** 4 1/2

Country-Style Ribs and Sauerkraut

5 servings

SLOW COOKER:
3 1/2- to 4-quart

PREP TIME:
10 minutes

COOK TIME:
Low 8 to 10 hours

Betty's Success Tip

Sauerkraut sometimes can be quite salty. Do a quick taste test before adding it to the slow cooker. If you find it too salty, rinse it in a strainer under cold water, then drain well.

Serving Suggestion

Serve this German-inspired entrée with plenty of rye bread and butter. Offer mugs of cold beer to the adults and apple cider to the kids.

2 pounds pork boneless country-style ribs

1 medium cooking apple, sliced

1 small onion, sliced

1 can (16 ounces) sauerkraut, rinsed and drained

3 tablespoons packed brown sugar

1 teaspoon caraway seed

1/4 cup dry white wine or apple juice

1. Place ribs, apple and onion in 3 1/2- to 4-quart slow cooker. Top with sauerkraut, brown sugar and caraway seed; mix lightly. Pour wine over top.

2. Cover and cook on low heat setting 8 to 10 hours until ribs are tender.

1 Serving: Calories 415 (Calories from Fat 190); Fat 21g (Saturated 7g); Cholesterol 10mg; Sodium 670mg; Carbohydrate 17g (Dietary Fiber 3g); Protein 38g • **% Daily Value:** Vitamin A 0%; Vitamin C 12%; Calcium 4%; Iron 16% • **Diet Exchanges:** 1 Starch, 4 1/2 Medium-Fat Meat • **Carbohydrate Choices:** 1

Asian Hoisin Ribs

4 servings

SLOW COOKER:
3 1/2- to 4-quart

PREP TIME:
10 minutes

COOK TIME:
Low 8 to 10 hours

Ingredient Substitution

The sesame oil adds a nice subtle sesame flavor to the ribs. However, if you don't have sesame oil, sprinkle the ribs with toasted sesame seed before serving.

Serving Suggestion

Serve these ribs with bowls of steaming rice and Chinese-style coleslaw. Finish the meal with fresh pineapple chunks sprinkled with chopped fresh mint.

3 pounds pork bone-in country-style ribs

1 medium onion, sliced

1/2 cup hoisin sauce

1/3 cup seasoned rice vinegar

1/4 cup soy sauce

1 tablespoon grated gingerroot or 1 teaspoon ground ginger

2 teaspoons sesame oil, if desired

Fresh cilantro leaves, if desired

1. Place ribs in 3 1/2- to 4-quart slow cooker. Cover with onion slices. Mix remaining ingredients except cilantro; pour over ribs and onion.

2. Cover and cook on low heat setting 8 to 10 hours or until ribs are tender.

3. Remove ribs to serving platter; keep warm. Skim fat from surface of juices in cooker. Serve ribs with sauce; sprinkle with cilantro.

1 Serving: Calories 450 (Calories from Fat 215); Fat 24g (Saturated 8g); Cholesterol 115mg; Sodium 1500 mg; Carbohydrate 18g (Dietary Fiber 2g); Protein 43g • **% Daily Value:** Vitamin A 10%; Vitamin C 4%; Calcium 4%; Iron 14% • **Diet Exchanges:** 1 Starch, 6 Lean Meat, 1 Fat • **Carbohydrate Choices:** 1

Asian Hoisin Ribs

Apricot-Glazed Pork Roast and Stuffing

6 servings

SLOW COOKER:
3 1/2- to 4-quart

PREP TIME:
10 minutes

COOK TIME:
Low 7 to 8 hours

Betty's Success Tip

To give this tasty roast more color, brown all sides in a tablespoon of vegetable oil in a 12-inch skillet over medium-high heat before brushing with the jam.

Ingredient Substitution

If you don't have any balsamic vinegar, use 1 tablespoon cider or white vinegar. Also, peach jam will work if apricot jam isn't readily available on your pantry shelf.

4 cups herb-seasoned stuffing cubes

3/4 cup chicken broth

1/2 cup dried apricots, chopped

1/3 cup frozen chopped onions (from 12-ounce bag)

2- to 2 1/2-pound pork boneless loin roast

1/3 cup apricot jam

1 tablespoon balsamic vinegar

1. Spray 3 1/2- to 4-quart slow cooker with cooking spray. Mix stuffing, broth, apricots and onions in cooker. Place pork on stuffing mixture. Mix jam and vinegar; brush over pork.

2. Cover and cook on low heat setting 7 to 8 hours or until pork is tender.

3. Remove pork from cooker; place on cutting board. Stir stuffing before serving. Cut pork into slices; serve with stuffing.

1 Serving: Calories 515 (Calories from Fat 125); Fat 14g (Saturated 5g); Cholesterol 95mg; Sodium 950mg; Carbohydrate 61g (Dietary Fiber 4g); Protein 40g • **% Daily Value:** Vitamin A 32%; Vitamin C 2%; Calcium 6%; Iron 22% • **Diet Exchanges:** 3 Starch, 4 Lean Meat, 1 Fruit • **Carbohydrate Choices:** 4

Apricot-Glazed Pork Roast and Stuffing

Green Chile and Pork Stew

6 servings

SLOW COOKER:
3 1/2- to 4-quart

PREP TIME:
20 minutes

COOK TIME:
Low 6 to 7 hours

Betty's Success Tip

An easy way to skim the fat from stews and soups is to place a slice of bread on top of the mixture for a few minutes to absorb the fat. Or, use a spoon to carefully remove any excess fat.

Serving Suggestion

Serve stew over biscuits to make 8 servings out of 6! Heat oven to 450°. Mix 2 1/4 cups Bisquick mix with 2/3 cup milk until soft dough forms. Drop dough by 8 spoonfuls onto ungreased cookie sheet. Bake about 10 minutes or until golden brown. Split a biscuit in half, and place both halves in bowl. Spoon stew over the top.

1 1/2-pound pork boneless loin, cut into cubes

2 cans (4 ounces each) whole green chiles, drained and cut into strips

1 jar (20 ounces) thick-and-chunky salsa

1 can (15 1/4 ounces) whole kernel corn, drained

1 can (15 ounces) garbanzo beans, rinsed and drained

1 medium onion, chopped (1/2 cup)

1 cup chicken broth

3 teaspoons chili powder

3 teaspoons dried cilantro leaves, if desired

2 teaspoons sugar

1. Mix all ingredients in 3 1/2- to 4-quart slow cooker.

2. Cover and cook on low heat setting at least 6 to 7 hours, or until pork is tender.

1 Serving: Calories 390 (Calories from Fat 110); Fat 12g (Saturated 4g); Cholesterol 70mg; Sodium 1040mg; Carbohydrate 44g (Dietary Fiber 10g); Protein 36g • **% Daily Value:** Vitamin A 28%; Vitamin C 28%; Calcium 8%; Iron 28% • **Diet Exchanges:** 3 Starch, 3 Lean Meat • **Carbohydrate Choices:** 3

Ham with Fruit Chutney

8 servings

SLOW COOKER:
3 1/2- to 4-quart

PREP TIME:
5 minutes

COOK TIME:
Low 6 to 8 hours

Serving Suggestion

Serve this easy-to-make ham and fruit chutney with steamed small red potatoes, cooked asparagus spears and crusty sourdough dinner rolls with butter.

Finishing Touch

Spoon fruit chutney into a clear glass bowl and place in the center of a decorative glass platter. Arrange ham slices around the chutney. A jar of colorful spiced crab apples and sprigs of Italian parsley tucked around the ham make a pretty garnish.

3-pound fully cooked smoked boneless ham

1/4 teaspoon pepper

2 jars (6 ounces each) fruit chutney (1 1/2 cups)

1 cup dried fruit and raisin mixture (from 6-ounce bag), chopped

1 cup frozen small whole onions (from 1-pound bag)

1 tablespoon balsamic vinegar

1. Place ham in 3 1/2- to 4-quart slow cooker. Sprinkle with pepper. Mix remaining ingredients; pour over ham.

2. Cover and cook on low heat setting 6 to 8 hours or until ham is hot.

3. Remove ham from cooker; place on cutting board. Stir fruit chutney before serving. Cut ham into slices; serve with fruit chutney.

1 Serving: Calories 395 (Calories from Fat 145); Fat 16g (Saturated 5g); Cholesterol 100mg; Sodium 2580mg; Carbohydrate 26g (Dietary Fiber 2g); Protein 39g • **% Daily Value:** Vitamin A 8%; Vitamin C 4%; Calcium 2%; Iron 16% • **Diet Exchanges:** 5 Lean Meat, 2 Fruit • **Carbohydrate Choices:** 2

Ham with Cheesy Potatoes

8 servings

SLOW COOKER:
5- to 6-quart

PREP TIME:
5 minutes

COOK TIME:
Low 5 to 6 hours

Ingredient Substitution

For a delicious, cheesy potato side dish, omit the ham. It's a great side to serve with roasted chicken, pork chops or loin roast.

Serving Suggestion

Serve this comfort-food favorite with cooked broccoli spears and crisp wedges of iceberg lettuce drizzled with French or ranch dressing.

1 bag (28 ounces) frozen diced potatoes with onions and peppers, thawed

2 cups shredded Cheddar and Monterey Jack cheese blend (8 ounces)

1 can (10 3/4 ounces) condensed cream of celery soup

1 container (8 ounces) sour cream

3-pound fully cooked smoked boneless ham

1. Spray 5- to 6-quart slow cooker with cooking spray. Mix frozen potatoes, cheese, soup and sour cream in cooker. Cut ham lengthwise in half; place ham on potato mixture.

2. Cover and cook on low heat setting 5 to 6 hours or until potatoes are tender.

3. Remove ham from cooker; place on cutting board. Gently stir potatoes well before serving. Cut ham into slices; serve with potatoes.

1 Serving: Calories 665 (Calories from Fat 370); Fat 41g (Saturated 17g); Cholesterol 150mg; Sodium 3320mg; Carbohydrate 28g (Dietary Fiber 3g); Protein 49g • **% Daily Value:** Vitamin A 12%; Vitamin C 16%; Calcium 24%; Iron 16% • **Diet Exchanges:** 1 Starch, 5 Medium-Fat Meat, 1 Milk • **Carbohydrate Choices:** 2

Ham with Cheesy Potatoes

Ham and Lentil Stew

10 servings

SLOW COOKER:
5- to 6-quart

PREP TIME:
15 minutes

COOK TIME:
Low 8 to 10 hours

Betty's Success Tip

When it comes to slow cooking, lentils are a nice alternative to dried beans. Unlike beans, lentils don't require soaking before cooking—saving you even more time!

Finishing Touch

For extra crunch, top this homey lentil stew with canned shoestring potatoes. Pass a bottle of red pepper sauce or ground red pepper for those who like their stew a little hotter.

1 pound fully cooked smoked ham, cut into 1/2-inch cubes (3 cups)

4 medium stalks celery, chopped (2 cups)

4 medium carrots, chopped (2 cups)

1 large onion, chopped (1 cup)

2 cans (10 1/2 ounces each) condensed chicken broth

2 cups dried lentils (1 pound), sorted and rinsed

4 cups water

1. Mix all ingredients in 5- to 6-quart slow cooker.

2. Cover and cook on low heat setting 8 to 10 hours or until lentils are tender.

1 Serving: Calories 195 (Calories from Fat 45); Fat 5g (Saturated 2g); Cholesterol 25mg; Sodium 1080mg; Carbohydrate 26g (Dietary Fiber 10g); Protein 23g • **% Daily Value:** Vitamin A 90%; Vitamin C 4%; Calcium 4%; Iron 26% • **Diet Exchanges:** 1 1/2 Starch, 2 1/2 Very Lean Meat • **Carbohydrate Choices:** 2

Ham and Lentil Stew

Meaty Main Dishes

4

- Sweet-and-Sour Chicken 94
- Brazilian Saffron Chicken and Rice 96
- Garlic Chicken with Italian Beans 98
- Spicy Chicken in Peanut Sauce 100
- Turkey Teriyaki 101
- Beef Roast with Shiitake Mushroom Sauce 102
- Beef and Asparagus Over Noodles 104
- Chinese Beef and Broccoli 105
- Asian BBQ Beef Brisket 106
- Corned Beef and Cabbage Dinner 108
- Pot Roast–Style Beef Steak 110
- Savory Beef Short Rib Dinner 112
- Slow-Simmered Spaghetti Meat Sauce 113
- Italian Meatballs with Marinara Sauce 114
- Beef and Creamy Potato Casserole 116
- Hunter's-Style Pork Roast 117
- Mexican Pork Roast with Chili Sauce 118
- Cheesy Pork Quesadillas 120
- Spicy Pork and Pineapple Salad 121
- Barbecued Pork Chops 122
- Savory Barbecued Ribs 124
- Honey-Dijon Ham 126
- Supper Ham Frittata 128
- Ham and Asparagus Chowder 129

◀ **Savory Beef Short Rib Dinner (page 112)**

Sweet-and-Sour Chicken

6 servings

SLOW COOKER:
3 1/2- to 4-quart

PREP TIME:
10 minutes

COOK TIME:
Low 6 to 7 hours

FINISHING COOK TIME:
High 45 to 60 minutes

Betty's Success Tip

Sweet-and-sour sauces come in a variety of colors, ranging from pink to golden. The golden-colored variety will give this dish the most attractive look. Some sweet-and-sour sauces turn chicken an unsightly bright pink!

Serving Suggestion

There are several types of rice available. You may want to serve this sweet-and-sour dish over brown rice or jasmine rice for a change of pace. For dessert, serve orange sherbet drizzled with chocolate sauce along with coconut cookies.

1 1/2 cups baby-cut carrots

6 large boneless, skinless chicken thighs (about 2 pounds)

1/2 teaspoon crushed red pepper flakes

1 1/3 cups sweet-and-sour sauce

1 can (20 ounces) pineapple chunks in juice, drained

1 bag (1 pound) frozen stir-fry bell peppers and onions, thawed and drained

6 cups hot cooked rice

1. Place carrots in 3 1/2- to 4-quart slow cooker. Top with chicken; sprinkle with red pepper.

2. Cover and cook on low heat setting 6 to 7 hours or until juice of chicken is no longer pink when center of thickest pieces are cut.

3. Remove chicken from cooker; drain and discard liquid from cooker. Return chicken to cooker. Pour sweet-and-sour sauce over chicken; top with pineapple and stir-fry vegetables. Cover and cook on high heat setting 45 to 60 minutes or until carrots are tender. Serve with rice.

1 Serving: Calories 510 (Calories from Fat 80); Fat 9g (Saturated 3g); Cholesterol 55mg; Sodium 270mg; Carbohydrate 82g (Dietary Fiber 4g); Protein 25g • **% Daily Value:** Vitamin A 100%; Vitamin C 46%; Calcium 8%; Iron 26% • **Diet Exchanges:** 3 Starch, 2 Lean Meat, 2 Fruit, 1 Vegetable • **Carbohydrate Choices:** 5 1/2

Sweet-and-Sour Chicken

Brazilian Saffron Chicken and Rice

6 servings

SLOW COOKER:
3 1/2- to 4-quart

PREP TIME:
20 minutes

COOK TIME:
Low 5 to 6 hours

FINISHING COOK TIME:
High 1 hour

Betty's Success Tip

Sometimes bone-in chicken pieces become so tender during cooking that the meat separates and falls from the bone. If this happens, just pick out the bones before serving.

Ingredient Substitution

If you're having a hard time finding yellow rice mix at your grocery store, use an 8-ounce package of chicken-flavored rice mix and 1/4 teaspoon ground turmeric instead.

3- to 3 1/2-pound cut-up broiler-fryer chicken

3/4 teaspoon garlic salt

1 tablespoon olive or vegetable oil

1/2 cup chopped fully cooked smoked ham (3 ounces)

1 medium onion, chopped (1/2 cup)

1 medium red bell pepper, chopped (1 cup)

1 can (14 ounces) chicken broth

1 package (8 ounces) yellow rice mix

1/3 cup sliced pimiento-stuffed olives

1. Sprinkle chicken with garlic salt. Heat oil in 12-inch skillet over medium-high heat. Cook chicken in oil until brown on all sides; drain. Place chicken in 3 1/2- to 4-quart slow cooker. Top with ham, onion and bell pepper. Add broth.

2. Cover and cook on low heat setting 5 to 6 hours until juice of chicken is no longer pink when centers of thickest pieces are cut.

3. Remove chicken from cooker. Stir rice mix (dry) into mixture in cooker; return chicken to cooker. Cover and cook on high heat setting about 1 hour or until rice is tender. Serve chicken and rice with olives.

1 Serving: Calories 430 (Calories from Fat 145); Fat 16g (Saturated 5g); Cholesterol 95mg; Sodium 930mg; Carbohydrate 36g (Dietary Fiber 1g); Protein 35g • **% Daily Value:** Vitamin A 26%; Vitamin C 32%; Calcium 4%; Iron 18% • **Diet Exchanges:** 2 Starch, 4 Lean Meat, 1 Vegetable, 1/2 Fat • **Carbohydrate Choices:** 2 1/2

Brazilian Saffron Chicken and Rice

Garlic Chicken with Italian Beans

4 servings

SLOW COOKER:
3 1/2- to 4-quart

PREP TIME:
20 minutes

COOK TIME:
Low 7 to 8 hours

FINISHING COOK TIME:
Low 15 minutes

Ingredient Substitution

If you find your pantry bare when you go to look for diced tomatoes with balsamic vinegar, basil and olive oil, use diced tomatoes with Italian herbs instead.

Serving Suggestion

Serve this Italian-inspired dish with chunks of crusty Italian bread, and provide small bowls of olive oil for dipping. Add steamed broccoli spears for a tasty and colorful meal.

8 large chicken thighs and drumsticks (about 2 pounds)

1/2 teaspoon salt

1/4 teaspoon pepper

1 tablespoon olive or vegetable oil

1 medium bulb garlic, separated into cloves and peeled (about 15 cloves)

1 can (14 1/2 ounces) diced tomatoes with balsamic vinegar, basil and olive oil, undrained

1/2 cup chicken broth

2 cans (15 1/2 ounces each) great northern beans, rinsed and drained

Basil pesto, if desired

1. Sprinkle chicken with salt and pepper. Heat oil in 12-inch skillet over medium-high heat. Cook chicken in oil over medium-high heat until brown on all sides; drain.

2. Place chicken and garlic in 3 1/2- to 4-quart slow cooker. Pour tomatoes and broth over chicken.

3. Cover and cook on low heat setting 7 to 8 hours or until chicken is no longer pink when centers of thickest pieces are cut.

4. Remove chicken from cooker; keep warm. Skim fat from surface of juices in cooker. Stir in beans; cover and cook on low heat setting about 15 minutes or until heated through. Serve chicken with beans and pesto.

1 Serving: Calories 700 (Calories from Fat 260); Fat 29g (Saturated 7g); Cholesterol 130mg; Sodium 690mg; Carbohydrate 61g (Dietary Fiber 15g); Protein 64g • **% Daily Value:** Vitamin A 12%; Vitamin C 14%; Calcium 28%; Iron 64% • **Diet Exchanges:** 4 Starch, 7 Lean Meat • **Carbohydrate Choices:** 4

Garlic Chicken with Italian Beans

Spicy Chicken in Peanut Sauce

4 servings

SLOW COOKER:
4- to 5-quart

PREP TIME:
15 minutes

COOK TIME:
Low 7 to 8 hours

Betty's Success Tip

This dish, with many ingredients reminiscent of North African cooking, has a mellow, warm, spicy flavor and gets a burst of heat from the tomatoes with green chilies.

Serving Suggestion

Pass small bowls of roasted peanuts and chopped fresh cilantro to sprinkle over the chicken. Add warm pita bread wedges and baby carrots to round out the meal. For a sweet ending, dish up scoops of frozen yogurt.

1 tablespoon olive or vegetable oil

8 large chicken thighs (about 3 pounds), skin removed

1 large onion, chopped (1 cup)

2 cans (14 1/2 ounces each) diced tomatoes with green chilies, undrained

1 can (14 1/2 ounces) crushed tomatoes, undrained

2 tablespoons honey

1 1/2 teaspoons ground cumin

1 teaspoon ground cinnamon

1/3 cup creamy peanut butter

2 cups hot cooked couscous

1. Heat oil in 12-inch nonstick skillet over medium-high heat. Cook chicken in oil about 4 minutes, turning once, until brown.

2. Mix onion, diced and crushed tomatoes, honey, cumin and cinnamon in 4- to-5-quart slow cooker. Place chicken in slow cooker. Spoon tomato mixture over chicken.

3. Cover and cook on low heat setting 7 to 8 hours until juice of chicken is no longer pink when centers of thickest pieces are cut.

4. Stir in peanut butter until melted and well blended. Serve chicken and sauce over couscous.

1 Serving: Calories 670 (Calories from Fat 290); Fat 32g (Saturated 8g); Cholesterol 115mg; Sodium 890mg; Carbohydrate 51g (Dietary Fiber 7g); Protein 51g • **% Daily Value:** Vitamin A 24%; Vitamin C 32%; Calcium 16%; Iron 32% • **Diet Exchanges:** 3 Starch, 6 Lean Meat, 1 Vegetable, 1 1/2 Fat • **Carbohydrate Choices:** 3 1/2

Turkey Teriyaki

4 servings

SLOW COOKER:
3 1/2- to 4-quart

PREP TIME:
15 minutes

COOK TIME:
Low 9 to 10 hours

FINISHING COOK TIME:
Microwave 2 minutes

Betty's Success Tip

A "teriyaki" recipe simply means it has a marinade made from a mixture of soy sauce, sake (or sherry), sugar, ginger and seasonings. Beef, chicken and fish are commonly used, but you can add a tasty twist to this Japanese-inspired dish by using turkey.

Ingredient Substitution

Fresh gingerroot tastes best in this dish, but if you're out, use ground ginger instead. You can use 1/4 to 1/2 teaspoon of the dried spice in place of the fresh seasoning.

2 bone-in turkey thighs (about 2 pounds), skin removed

1/2 cup teriyaki baste and glaze (from 12-ounce bottle)

2 tablespoons orange marmalade

1/2 teaspoon grated gingerroot

1 clove garlic, finely chopped

1 tablespoon water

2 teaspoons cornstarch

1. Spray 3 1/2- to 4-quart slow cooker with cooking spray. Place turkey in slow cooker. Mix teriyaki glaze, marmalade, gingerroot and garlic; spoon over turkey. Turn turkey to coat with teriyaki mixture.

2. Cover and cook on low heat setting 9 to 10 hours or until juice of turkey is no longer pink when centers of thickest pieces are cut.

3. About 10 minutes before serving, remove turkey from cooker; place on serving platter. Remove and discard bones; cut turkey into serving pieces.

4. Mix water and cornstarch in 2-cup glass measuring cup or small microwavable bowl until smooth. Pour juices from cooker into cornstarch mixture; mix well. Microwave uncovered on High 1 to 2 minutes, stirring once halfway through cooking, until mixture boils and thickens slightly. Serve sauce with turkey.

1 Serving: Calories 255 (Calories from Fat 45); Fat 5g (Saturated 2g); Cholesterol 140mg; Sodium 1480mg; Carbohydrate 14g (Dietary Fiber 0g); Protein 38g • **% Daily Value:** Vitamin A 0%; Vitamin C 0%; Calcium 4%; Iron 20% • **Diet Exchanges:** 1 Starch, 5 Lean Meat • **Carbohydrate Choices:** 1

Beef Roast with Shiitake Mushroom Sauce

5 servings, with leftovers

SLOW COOKER:
3 1/2- to 4-quart

PREP TIME:
20 minutes

COOK TIME:
Low 8 to 10 hours

FINISHING COOK TIME:
Microwave 3 minutes

Betty's Success Tip

To clean mushrooms, brush them with a soft vegetable brush and then wipe clean with a damp cloth. Don't run mushrooms under water or their texture will become mushy.

Ingredient Substitution

Fresh shiitake mushrooms add a wonderful, rich flavor to this beef roast, but if they aren't available, you can use 2 cups sliced regular white mushrooms instead.

3 1/2 ounces fresh shiitake mushrooms, sliced

4-pound beef boneless rump or tip roast, trimmed of fat

1/4 cup hoisin sauce

2 cloves garlic, finely chopped

1/2 teaspoon salt

1/4 cup water

2 tablespoons cornstarch

2 medium green onions, sliced (2 tablespoons)

1. Place mushrooms in 3 1/2- to 4-quart slow cooker. Top with beef. Spread hoisin sauce over beef; sprinkle with garlic and salt.

2. Cover and cook on low heat setting 8 to 10 hours or until beef is tender.

3. About 10 minutes before serving, remove beef from cooker; place on serving platter and cover to keep warm. Mix water and cornstarch in 4-cup glass measuring cup or medium microwavable bowl until smooth. Pour juices from cooker into cornstarch mixture; mix well. Microwave uncovered on High 2 to 3 minutes, stirring once halfway through cooking, until mixture boils and thickens slightly.

4. Cut roast in half; set one half aside. Cut remaining half into slices; place on serving platter. Remove 1 1/2 cups sauce and set aside. Spoon some of the remaining sauce over beef slices. Sprinkle with onions. Serve with any remaining sauce.

5. Divide reserved roast into 2 portions. Slice each; cut slices into 2 × 1/4-inch strips. Divide strips evenly into 2 plastic storage containers with lids. Add 1 cup sauce to 1 container; cover and label for Beef and Asparagus Over Noodles (page 104). Add 1/2 cup sauce to other container; cover and label for Chinese Beef and Broccoli (page 105). Refrigerate both containers up to 3 days or freeze up to 2 months for later use. If frozen, thaw in refrigerator before using.

1 Serving: Calories 225 (Calories from Fat 55); Fat 6g (Saturated 6g); Cholesterol 95mg; Sodium 340mg; Carbohydrate 9g (Dietary Fiber 1g); Protein 37g • **% Daily Value:** Vitamin A 4%; Vitamin C 2%; Calcium 2%; Iron 40% • **Diet Exchanges:** 5 Very Lean Meat, 1 Fat • **Carbohydrate Choices:** 1/2

Beef Roast with Shiitake Mushroom Sauce

Beef and Asparagus Over Noodles

4 servings

PREP TIME:
15 minutes

COOK TIME:
15 minutes

Betty's Success Tip

The peak season for asparagus is February to June. Watch for it at your local farmers' market and supermarkets, and choose stalks that are bright green and firm with tight tips.

Serving Suggestion

Make a package of roasted garlic mashed potatoes instead of cooking noodles to serve with this easy skillet dish.

3 cups uncooked medium egg noodles (6 ounces)

2 cups 1 1/2-inch pieces fresh asparagus spears

1/2 cup water

1 container cooked Beef Roast with Shiitake Mushroom Sauce (page 102) for Beef and Asparagus over Noodles, thawed if frozen

1 1/2 teaspoons Worcestershire sauce

1/8 teaspoon pepper

1 container (8 ounces) sour cream (1 cup)

1. Cook and drain noodles as directed on package.

2. While noodles are cooking, heat asparagus and water to boiling in 10-inch skillet over high heat; reduce heat to medium. Cover and cook 3 to 4 minutes or until asparagus is crisp-tender. Stir in beef roast strips with sauce, Worcestershire sauce and pepper. Cover and cook 3 to 4 minutes or until thoroughly heated.

3. Stir sour cream into beef mixture. Cover and cook 3 to 4 minutes, stirring frequently, until thoroughly heated. Serve over noodles.

➤ what a **Great Idea**...with Leftovers

1 Serving: Calories 425 (Calories from Fat 155); Fat 17g (Saturated 8g); Cholesterol 135mg; Sodium 430mg; Carbohydrate 36g (Dietary Fiber 2g); Protein 32g • **% Daily Value:** Vitamin A 22%; Vitamin C 14%; Calcium 8%; Iron 24% • **Diet Exchanges:** 2 1/2 Starch, 3 1/2 Lean Meat, 1 Fat • **Carbohydrate Choices:** 2 1/2

Chinese Beef and Broccoli

4 servings

PREP TIME:
5 minutes

COOK TIME:
10 minutes

Betty's Success Tip

Soy sauce, a common ingredient in Chinese and Japanese cuisine, is made from soybeans, wheat, yeast and salt. There are a number of varieties of soy sauce, which vary in color, texture and taste. Soy sauce lasts for a long time and it's best to store it in a cool dark place at room temperature.

Serving Suggestion

Here's a fun way to serve rice. Spray the inside of a 1/2-cup measuring cup with cooking spray. For each serving, press hot rice into the cup. Place the cup upside down in the bottom of a bowl, and unmold the rice. Spoon the beef mixture around the mound of rice.

2 cups uncooked instant rice

2 1/4 cups water

1 container cooked Beef Roast with Shiitake Mushroom Sauce (page 102) for Chinese Beef and Broccoli, thawed if frozen

1/4 cup soy sauce

1/4 teaspoon ground ginger

1 bag (14 ounces) frozen broccoli flowerets

1. Cook rice in 2 cups of the water as directed on package.

2. While rice is cooking, mix beef roast strips with sauce, remaining 1/4 cup water, the soy sauce and ginger in 10-inch skillet. Heat to boiling over medium–high heat; stir in frozen broccoli. Cover and cook 5 to 6 minutes, stirring once, until broccoli is tender. Serve over rice.

➤ what a **Great Idea**...with Leftovers

1 Serving: Calories 375 (Calories from Fat 35); Fat 4g (Saturated 1g); Cholesterol 60mg; Sodium 1660mg; Carbohydrate 54g (Dietary Fiber 3g); Protein 31g • **% Daily Value:** Vitamin A 32%; Vitamin C 30%; Calcium 6%; Iron 28% • **Diet Exchanges:** 3 Starch, 3 Very Lean Meat, 1/2 Fat • **Carbohydrate Choices:** 3 1/2

Asian BBQ Beef Brisket

8 servings

SLOW COOKER:
3 1/2- to 4-quart

PREP TIME:
20 minutes

COOK TIME:
Low 9 to 11 hours

Betty's Success Tip

Be sure to use fresh beef brisket instead of a "corned" beef brisket. Corned beef brisket has been cured in seasoned brine, which may be too strong a flavor for this dish.

Ingredient Substitution

If you can't find fresh beef brisket, cooking the same cut of meat you use for a pot roast, such as beef boneless bottom roast or chuck roast, will also work.

1 tablespoon vegetable oil

3-pound fresh beef brisket (not corned beef)

3/4 cup barbecue sauce

3/4 cup teriyaki baste and glaze (from 12-ounce bottle)

1 small onion, chopped (1/4 cup)

1 to 2 chipotle chilies in adobo sauce (from 7-ounce can), finely chopped

1. Heat oil in 12-inch skillet over medium-high heat. Cook beef in oil until brown on both sides. Place beef in 3 1/2- to 4-quart slow cooker. Mix remaining ingredients; pour over beef.

2. Cover and cook on low heat setting 9 to 11 hours until beef is tender.

3. Remove beef from cooker; place on cutting board. Cut beef across grain into thin slices. Skim fat from sauce in cooker. Serve sauce with beef.

1 Serving: Calories 345 (Calories from Fat 125); Fat 14g (Saturated 5g); Cholesterol 95mg; Sodium 1400mg; Carbohydrate 14g (Dietary Fiber 0g); Protein 38g • **% Daily Value:** Vitamin A 4%; Vitamin C 2%; Calcium 2%; Iron 20% • **Diet Exchanges:** 1 Starch, 5 Lean Meat • **Carbohydrate Choices:** 1

Finishing Touches

You can dress up your favorite slow cooker dishes with a little taste twist or fun garnish. Here are some "sprinkles" that will add crunch, color and an extra flavor boost.

Sprinkle Casseroles and Soups with . . .

- Toasted nuts
- Toasted sesame seed
- Crushed unsweetened cereal mixed with dried herbs
- Crushed tortilla or corn chips mixed with grated Parmesan cheese and parsley
- Toasted pumpkin seeds or sunflower nuts
- Cheese-flavored fish-shaped crackers

Top Chicken Dishes and Stews with . . .

- Chutney
- Pesto
- Plain yogurt mixed with finely chopped cucumber
- Chunky salsa
- Chopped fresh chives
- Chopped fresh rosemary leaves

Spoon on Chilies . . .

- Guacamole
- Sour cream mixed with lime juice
- Shredded Cheddar or Monterey Jack cheese
- Crushed corn or tortilla chips, plain or flavored
- Thick-and-chunky salsa
- Chopped fresh cilantro
- Chopped fresh vegetables such as tomatoes, green onion, avocado, onion and jicama

Top Beef Dishes and Stews with . . .

- Crushed herb-flavored seasoned croutons
- Canned French-fried onions
- Chopped tomatoes and avocados
- Pine nuts or coarsely chopped walnuts
- Crumbled crispy cooked bacon or bacon bits
- Chunky salsa

Soup's On!

Tired of dipping the same old saltines in your soup? For a finishing flavor flourish, serve one of these tasty tidbits the next time you serve soup from your slow cooker.

- **Melt** slices of Brie cheese on crackers or on thin slices of French bread and top with toasted sliced almonds.
- **Blend** whipped cream cheese with finely chopped green onions and parsley to spread on crackers or dollop on soup.
- **Sprinkle** shredded Monterey Jack or hot pepper Jack on flour or corn tortillas and add a spoonful of salsa. Roll up

and microwave on High for 20 to 30 seconds or until cheese is melted.

- **Dust** sesame seed over slices of buttered bread and broil briefly (or use a toaster oven's "top brown" feature) until the butter is melted and sesame seed is golden. Cut into triangles to serve.

Corned Beef and Cabbage Dinner

8 servings

SLOW COOKER:
5- to 6 1/2-quart

PREP TIME:
15 minutes

COOK TIME:
Low 10 to 12 hours

FINISHING COOK TIME:
High 30 to 35 minutes

Betty's Success Tip

To keep cabbage wedges whole, don't remove the core from the cabbage; just cut through it so a bit of the core holds each wedge together.

Serving Suggestion

Pile leftover corned beef and cabbage on slices of toasted rye bread, and spread with apple mustard. Top the sandwich filling with a slice of Swiss cheese, and heat it under the broiler until the cheese melts and bubbles.

2 pounds small red potatoes

1 1/2 cups baby-cut carrots

1 medium onion, cut into 8 wedges

2- to 2 1/2-pound well-trimmed corned beef brisket with seasoning packet

2 cups apple juice

Water

8 thin wedges cabbage

Horseradish Sauce (below)

1. Place potatoes, carrots and onion in 5- to 6 1/2-quart slow cooker. Thoroughly rinse beef; place on top of vegetables. Sprinkle beef with contents of seasoning packet. Add apple juice and just enough water to cover beef.

2. Cover and cook on low heat setting 10 to 12 hours until beef is tender.

3. Remove beef from cooker; place on serving platter and cover to keep warm. Add cabbage wedges to vegetables and broth in cooker. Cover and cook on high heat setting 30 to 35 minutes or until cabbage is crisp-tender.

4. Make Horseradish Sauce. Cut beef across grain into thin slices. Remove vegetables from slow cooker, using slotted spoon. Serve beef and vegetables with sauce.

Horseradish Sauce

1/2 cup sour cream

1/4 cup mayonnaise or salad dressing

2 tablespoons prepared horseradish

2 teaspoons Dijon mustard

Mix all ingredients.

1 Serving: Calories 430 (Calories from Fat 215); Fat 24g (Saturated 8g); Cholesterol 90mg; Sodium 1040mg; Carbohydrate 41g (Dietary Fiber 6g); Protein 19g • **% Daily Value:** Vitamin A 100%; Vitamin C 38%; Calcium 8%; Iron 20% • **Diet Exchanges:** 2 Starch, 1 1/2 High-Fat Meat, 2 Vegetable, 2 Fat • **Carbohydrate Choices:** 3

Corned Beef and Cabbage Dinner

Pot Roast–Style Beef Steak

4 servings

SLOW COOKER:
3 1/2- to 4-quart

PREP TIME:
25 minutes

COOK TIME:
Low 8 to 10 hours

FINISHING COOKING TIME:
5 minutes

Betty's Success Tip

Get a head start on preparing this dish by cutting up the carrots and onion the night before. Wrap in plastic wrap or put in covered plastic containers and refrigerate. Potatoes will turn brown, so peel and cut them just before adding to the slow cooker.

Serving Suggestion

Pair this beef steak and vegetable dish with a hearty cracked wheat bread, perfect for dipping into the rich, flavorful gravy.

1 1/2 pounds beef boneless top round steak (1/2 inch thick)

1 tablespoon all-purpose flour

1/2 teaspoon salt

1/8 teaspoon pepper

4 medium potatoes, peeled and each cut into 6 pieces

4 large carrots, cut into 1-inch pieces

1 medium onion, thinly sliced

1 dried bay leaf

1 can (14 ounces) beef broth

1 teaspoon Worcestershire sauce

2 tablespoons cornstarch

1. Cut beef into 4 equal pieces. Mix flour, salt and pepper in shallow bowl. Add beef pieces; turn to coat both sides.

2. Spray 12-inch nonstick skillet with cooking spray; heat over medium-high heat. Cook beef in skillet 4 to 6 minutes, turning once, until brown.

3. Mix potatoes, carrots and onion in 3 1/2- to 4-quart slow cooker. Add bay leaf. Place beef on vegetables. Mix 1 1/2 cups of the beef broth (reserve remaining broth) and Worcestershire sauce; pour over beef.

4. Cover and cook on low heat setting 8 to 10 hours or until beef is tender.

5. About 5 minutes before serving, remove beef and vegetables from cooker, using slotted spoon; place on serving platter. Cover to keep warm.

6. Pour liquid from cooker into 1 1/2-quart saucepan; remove bay leaf. Mix reserved beef broth and the cornstarch in small bowl until smooth. Stir into liquid in saucepan. Heat to boiling over medium-high heat, stirring constantly. Boil and stir 1 minute. Serve sauce with beef and vegetables.

1 Serving: Calories 370 (Calories from Fat 55); Fat 6g (Saturated 2g); Cholesterol 90mg; Sodium 860mg; Carbohydrate 40g (Dietary Fiber 4g); Protein 39g • **% Daily Value:** Vitamin A 100%; Vitamin C 14%; Calcium 4%; Iron 24% • **Diet Exchanges:** 2 Starch, 4 1/2 Very Lean Meat, 1 Fat • **Carbohydrate Choices:** 2 1/2

Pot Roast-Style Beef Steak

Savory Beef Short Rib Dinner

4 servings

Photo on page 92

SLOW COOKER:
4- to 6-quart

PREP TIME:
35 minutes

COOK TIME:
Low 8 to 10 hours

FINISHING COOK TIME:
Microwave 4 minutes

Betty's Success Tip

This recipe calls for dry sun-dried tomatoes, which absorb juices and become tender during cooking. Don't confuse them with oil-packed sun-dried tomatoes. Look for dry sun-dried tomatoes in the produce department near the other dried foods.

Ingredient Substitution

To cut down on prep time, use 16 baby-cut carrots instead of the whole carrots.

2 pounds beef short ribs

1/2 large onion, cut into 4 wedges

2 sun-dried tomato halves (not oil-packed), cut into thin strips

4 medium carrots, cut lengthwise in half, then cut crosswise in half

8 small red potatoes (1 pound)

1 clove garlic, finely chopped

1/2 teaspoon salt

1/2 teaspoon dried thyme leaves

1/2 teaspoon dried basil leaves

1/4 teaspoon pepper

1/2 cup dry red wine or water

1 cup water

1 teaspoon beef bouillon granules

2 tablespoons all-purpose flour

1. Cook ribs in 12-inch nonstick skillet over medium-high heat, turning frequently, until brown on all sides. While ribs are browning, layer onion, tomatoes, carrots, potatoes and garlic in 4- to 6-quart slow cooker.

2. Place ribs on vegetables in cooker. Sprinkle ribs with salt, thyme, basil and pepper. Drain off any fat from skillet; add wine, 1/2 cup of the water and the bouillon to skillet. Heat to boiling over medium heat, stirring occasionally. Pour hot wine mixture over ribs.

3. Cover and cook on low heat setting 8 to 10 hours or until ribs are tender.

4. About 15 minutes before serving, remove ribs and vegetables, using slotted spoon; place in serving bowl. Skim fat from juices in cooker.

5. Mix remaining 1/2 cup water and the flour in 4-cup glass measuring cup or medium microwavable bowl until smooth. Pour juices from cooker into flour mixture; mix well. Microwave uncovered on High 3 to 4 minutes, stirring once halfway through cooking, until mixture boils. Pour sauce over ribs and vegetables.

1 Serving: Calories 425 (Calories from Fat 115); Fat 13g (Saturated 5g); Cholesterol 50mg; Sodium 710mg; Carbohydrate 55g (Dietary Fiber 6g); Protein 22g • **% Daily Value:** Vitamin A 100%; Vitamin C 24%; Calcium 4%; Iron 24% • **Diet Exchanges:** 3 Starch, 2 Medium-Fat Meat, 2 Vegetable • **Carbohydrate Choices:** 3 1/2

Slow-Simmered Spaghetti Meat Sauce

8 servings

SLOW COOKER:
3 1/2- to 4-quart

PREP TIME:
20 minutes

COOK TIME:
Low 8 to 10 hours

Ingredient Substitution

A 1/2 pound of pork sausage can be used instead of the Italian sausage if it's more readily available. No fresh garlic? Use 1/4 teaspoon garlic powder or 1/2 teaspoon instant minced garlic instead.

Serving Suggestion

For a meal in a snap, serve with purchased garlic bread and a buy-in-the-bag Caesar salad mix. A slice of store-bought cheesecake is the perfect dessert.

1 pound lean ground beef

1/2 pound bulk Italian pork sausage

2 medium carrots, finely chopped (1 cup)

1 medium green bell pepper, chopped (1 cup)

1 medium onion, chopped (1/2 cup)

2 cloves garlic, finely chopped

1 can (28 ounces) crushed tomatoes, undrained

1 can (8 ounces) tomato sauce

1 can (6 ounces) tomato paste

1 tablespoon packed brown sugar

1 tablespoon dried Italian seasoning

1/2 teaspoon salt

1/4 teaspoon pepper

16 ounces uncooked spaghetti

Shredded fresh Parmesan cheese, if desired

1. Cook beef and sausage in 10-inch skillet over medium heat, stirring frequently, until beef is brown and sausage is no longer pink, about 8 minutes; drain.

2. Mix beef mixture and remaining ingredients except spaghetti and Parmesan cheese in 3 1/2- to 4-quart slow cooker.

3. Cover and cook on low heat setting 8 to 10 hours.

4. About 20 minutes before serving, cook and drain spaghetti as directed on package. Serve sauce with hot cooked spaghetti and Parmesan cheese.

1 Serving: Calories 440 (Calories from Fat 125); Fat 14g (Saturated 5g); Cholesterol 45mg; Sodium 850mg; Carbohydrate 62g (Dietary Fiber 5g); Protein 23g • **% Daily Value:** Vitamin A 72%; Vitamin C 36%; Calcium 8%; Iron 28% • **Diet Exchanges:** 3 1/2 Starch, 1/2 High-Fat Meat, 2 Vegetable, 1 1/2 Fat • **Carbohydrate Choices:** 4

Italian Meatballs with Marinara Sauce

6 servings (4 meatballs each)

SLOW COOKER:
3 1/2- to 4-quart

PREP TIME:
15 minutes

BAKE TIME:
35 minutes

COOK TIME:
Low 6 to 7 hours

Ingredient Substitution

Substitute any flavor of marinara or spaghetti sauce, such as herbed, sun-dried tomato or garlic and onion, to vary the flavor in this recipe.

Serving Suggestion

These meatballs make a great filling for sandwiches. Cut 8 small rustic sourdough or Italian rolls horizontally in half. Place 3 meatballs in each roll; top each sandwich with a 1-ounce slice of provolone cheese, and drizzle with marinara sauce.

3/4 pound ground beef

3/4 pound ground pork

1 small onion, chopped (1/4 cup)

2 cloves garlic, finely chopped

2 teaspoons Italian seasoning

1/4 cup Italian-style dry bread crumbs

1 egg, slightly beaten

1 jar (28 ounces) marinara sauce

1. Heat oven to 375°. Line jelly roll pan, 15 1/2 × 10 1/2 × 1 inch, with aluminum foil; spray with cooking spray. Mix beef, pork, onion, garlic, Italian seasoning, bread crumbs and egg. Shape mixture into twenty-four 1 1/2-inch balls. Place in pan. Bake 30 to 35 minutes or until no longer pink in center.

2. Place meatballs in 3 1/2- to 4-quart slow cooker. Pour marinara sauce over meatballs.

3. Cover and cook on low heat setting 6 to 7 hours to blend and develop flavors.

1 Serving: Calories 410 (Calories from Fat 200); Fat 22g (Saturated 7g); Cholesterol 105mg; Sodium 950mg; Carbohydrate 29g (Dietary Fiber 2g); Protein 24g • **% Daily Value:** Vitamin A 18%; Vitamin C 16%; Calcium 6%; Iron 16% • **Diet Exchanges:** 1 1/2 Starch, 2 1/2 High-Fat Meat, 1 Vegetable, 1 Fat • **Carbohydrate Choices:** 2

Italian Meatballs with Marinara Sauce

Beef and Creamy Potato Casserole

4 servings

SLOW COOKER:
3 1/2- to 4-quart

PREP TIME:
15 minutes

COOK TIME:
Low 6 to 7 hours

Ingredient Substitution

Used up the last of your cream of mushroom soup? Any flavor of condensed cream soup, such as cream of celery or chicken, will work fine as well.

Serving Suggestion

Serve this all-American, meat-and-potato dish with dinner rolls and a simple salad of tomato slices on salad greens, drizzled with your favorite salad dressing. Finish with chocolate brownies topped with a scoop of vanilla ice cream and a spoonful of hot fudge sauce.

1 pound lean ground beef

1 can (10 3/4 ounces) condensed cream of mushroom soup

1/2 cup milk

1/4 teaspoon pepper

1 can (2.8 ounces) French-fried onions

4 cups frozen country-style shredded hash brown potatoes (from 32-ounce bag)

2 cups frozen cut green beans

1. Cook beef in 10-inch skillet over medium heat about 8 minutes, stirring frequently, until brown; drain. Stir in soup, milk, pepper and half of the onions.

2. Spray 3 1/2- to 4-quart slow cooker with cooking spray. Layer potatoes and green beans in cooker. Top with beef mixture; spread evenly.

3. Cover and cook on low heat setting 6 to 7 hours. Top with remaining onions before serving.

1 Serving: Calories 615 (Calories from Fat 290); Fat 32g (Saturated 15g); Cholesterol 70mg; Sodium 1320mg; Carbohydrate 60g (Dietary Fiber 6g); Protein 29g • **% Daily Value:** Vitamin A 10%; Vitamin C 14%; Calcium 12%; Iron 20% • **Diet Exchanges:** 3 1/2 Starch, 2 1/2 Medium-Fat Meat, 1 Vegetable, 4 Fat • **Carbohydrate Choices:** 4

Hunter's-Style Pork Roast

8 servings

SLOW COOKER:
3 1/2- to 4-quart

PREP TIME:
10 minutes

COOK TIME:
Low 9 to 11 hours

FINISHING COOK TIME:
High 15 to 30 minutes

Betty's Success Tip

Cacciatore, a popular Italian dish also referred to as hunter's-style, usually contains thickened tomato gravy with mushrooms, tomatoes and other vegetables. Chicken Cacciatore is the most popular example, but pork makes a delicious change.

Ingredient Substitution

Hunter's gravy mix is a packaged gravy mix flavored with mushrooms and wine, but an envelope of any pork or beef gravy mix can be used instead.

2 1/2- to 3-pound pork boneless sirloin or loin roast

1 cup baby-cut carrots

2 cans (14 1/2 ounces each) diced tomatoes with roasted garlic, undrained

1 envelope (1 1/4 ounces) hunter's gravy mix

2 tablespoons all-purpose flour

2 tablespoons water

1 jar (4 1/2 ounces) sliced mushrooms, drained

1 package (8 or 9 ounces) frozen cut green beans, thawed and drained

1. Place pork in 3 1/2- to 4-quart slow cooker; top with carrots. Mix tomatoes and gravy mix (dry); pour over pork and carrots.

2. Cover and cook on low heat setting 9 to 11 hours or until pork is tender.

3. Remove pork and carrots to serving platter, using slotted spoon; cover with aluminum foil. Mix flour and water. Gradually stir flour mixture, mushrooms and green beans into liquid in cooker. Cover and cook on high heat setting 15 to 30 minutes or until slightly thickened. Serve sauce with pork and carrots.

1 Serving: Calories 265 (Calories from Fat 100); Fat 11g (Saturated 4g); Cholesterol 85mg; Sodium 450mg; Carbohydrate 12g (Dietary Fiber 3g); Protein 33g • **% Daily Value:** Vitamin A 66%; Vitamin C 14%; Calcium 6%; Iron 12% • **Diet Exchanges:** 4 Lean Meat, 2 Vegetables • **Carbohydrate Choices:** 1

Mexican Pork Roast with Chili Sauce

6 servings, with leftovers

SLOW COOKER:
4- to 6-quart

PREP TIME:
15 minutes

COOK TIME:
Low 8 to 10 hours

FINISHING COOK TIME:
Microwave 3 minutes

Betty's Success Tip

Chipotle chilies are actually dried, smoked jalapeños. In addition to being canned, they are also sold dried and pickled. Adobo sauce consists of ground chilies, herbs and vinegar. Look for chipotle chilies in adobo sauce in the Mexican-foods section of your supermarket.

Serving Suggestion

For a more casual meal, wrap the pork in a flour tortilla and top with the chili sauce.

1 medium onion, chopped (1/2 cup)

1 medium green bell pepper, chopped (1 cup)

4-pound pork boneless butt or shoulder roast, trimmed of fat

1 tablespoon packed brown sugar

2 tablespoons finely chopped chipotle chilies in adobo sauce (from 7-ounce can)

2 tablespoons ketchup

3/4 teaspoon salt

1 clove garlic, finely chopped

1/2 cup water

1/4 cup all-purpose flour

1. Place onion and bell pepper in 4- to 6-quart slow cooker. Top with pork roast. Mix brown sugar, chilies, ketchup, salt and garlic; spread over pork.

2. Cover and cook on low heat setting 8 to 10 hours or until pork is tender.

3. About 10 minutes before serving, remove pork from cooker; place on cutting board and cover to keep warm. Mix water and flour in 4-cup glass measuring cup or medium microwavable bowl until smooth. Pour juices from cooker into flour mixture; mix well. Microwave uncovered on High 2 to 3 minutes, stirring once halfway through cooking, until mixture boils and thickens slightly.

4. Cut pork in half; reserve one half of pork and 3/4 cup of the sauce. Cut remaining half of pork into slices; place on serving platter. Serve with remaining sauce.

5. Divide reserved pork into 2 portions. Shred 1 portion with 2 forks; place in plastic storage container with lid. Add 1/2 cup reserved sauce; cover and label for Cheesy Pork Quesadillas (page 120). Cut remaining portion of pork into 1/2-inch cubes; place in another plastic storage container with lid. Add 1/4 cup reserved sauce; cover and label for Spicy Pork and Pineapple Salad (page 121). Refrigerate both containers up to 3 days or freeze up to 2 months. If frozen, thaw in refrigerator before using.

1 Serving: Calories 330 (Calories from Fat 160); Fat 18g (Saturated 6g); Cholesterol 95mg; Sodium 370mg; Carbohydrate 9g (Dietary Fiber 0g); Protein 33g • **% Daily Value:** Vitamin A 4%; Vitamin C 16%; Calcium 2%; Iron 8% • **Diet Exchanges:** 1/2 Starch, 4 1/2 Lean Meat, 1 Fat • **Carbohydrate Choices:** 1/2

➤ what a **Great Idea...Leftovers**

Mexican Pork Roast with Chili Sauce

Cheesy Pork Quesadillas

4 sandwiches

PREP TIME:
5 minutes

COOK TIME:
12 minutes

Ingredient Substitution

Experiment with different kinds of cheese and flavors of salsa. Try Monterey Jack cheese with jalapeño peppers and garlic-flavored salsa, for example.

Serving Suggestion

These cheesy quesadillas make great appetizers. Make a double batch, and stack quesadillas on a decorative platter lined with napkins in festive colors. Let guests add their own quesadilla toppings such as guacamole, sour cream, lettuce, onions and tomatoes.

1 container cooked Mexican Pork Roast with Chili Sauce (page 118) for Cheesy Pork Quesadillas, thawed if frozen

1/4 cup sour cream

4 flour tortillas (10 to 12 inches in diameter)

1/2 cup thick-and-chunky salsa

4 slices (1 ounce each) Monterey Jack cheese, cut in half

1. Cook pork with sauce in 1 1/2-quart saucepan over medium-high heat, stirring occasionally, until heated.

2. Meanwhile, spread sour cream over half of each tortilla.

3. Top sour cream side of each tortilla with 1/2 cup pork mixture, 1 tablespoon salsa and 2 half-slices cheese. Fold tortilla over onto filling.

4. Spray 12-inch skillet with cooking spray; heat over medium-high heat. Cook 2 quesadillas at a time in skillet about 3 minutes, turning once, until filling is heated and tortillas are golden brown. Cut into wedges. Serve with remaining salsa.

➤ what a **Great Idea**...with Leftovers

1 Sandwich: Calories 590 (Calories from Fat 270); Fat 30g (Saturated 13g); Cholesterol 110mg; Sodium 760mg; Carbohydrate 42g (Dietary Fiber 2g); Protein 38g • **% Daily Value:** Vitamin A 14%; Vitamin C 8%; Calcium 32%; Iron 20% • **Diet Exchanges:** 3 Starch, 4 Lean Meat, 3 1/2 Fat • **Carbohydrate Choices:** 3

Spicy Pork and Pineapple Salad

4 servings

PREP TIME:
10 minutes

Ingredient Substitution

Canned pineapple is available crushed, or in chunks, slices or tidbits. Tidbits are already cut into little bite-size pieces, which work well for this recipe, but feel free to use other varieties if you have them on hand.

Serving Suggestion

To make this salad even more special, sprinkle with sliced green onions and toasted coconut, peanuts or cashew pieces.

1 can (8 ounces) pineapple tidbits in unsweetened juice

3 cups broccoli flowerets

1 container cooked Mexican Pork Roast with Chili Sauce (page 118) for Spicy Pork and Pineapple Salad, thawed if frozen

1/4 cup sour cream

2 tablespoons mayonnaise or salad dressing

1/4 teaspoon salt

Lettuce leaves, if desired

1. Drain pineapple tidbits, reserving 2 tablespoons juice. Mix broccoli, pork with sauce and pineapple in large bowl.

2. Mix reserved 2 tablespoons pineapple juice, the sour cream, mayonnaise and salt in small bowl with wire whisk. Pour over pork mixture; stir to coat. Serve on lettuce leaves.

➤ what a **Great Idea** ...with Leftovers

1 Serving: Calories 365 (Calories from Fat 200); Fat 22g (Saturated 7g); Cholesterol 85mg; Sodium 310mg; Carbohydrate 15g (Dietary Fiber 2g); Protein 27g • **% Daily Value:** Vitamin A 16%; Vitamin C 48%; Calcium 6%; Iron 8% • **Diet Exchanges:** 1/2 Starch, 3 1/2 Lean Meat, 1/2 Fruit, 2 Fat • **Carbohydrate Choices:** 1

Barbecued Pork Chops

4 servings

SLOW COOKER:
3 1/2- to 4-quart

PREP TIME:
10 minutes

COOK TIME:
Low 5 to 6 hours

FINISHING COOK TIME:
Microwave 2 minutes

4 pork boneless loin chops, 1 inch thick (about 3/4 pound), trimmed of fat

4 slices onion

1 clove garlic, finely chopped

3/4 cup barbecue sauce

1 tablespoon water

2 teaspoons cornstarch

1. Place pork chops in 3 1/2- to 4-quart slow cooker. Top each chop with onion slice and sprinkle with garlic. Pour barbecue sauce over chops.

2. Cover and cook on low heat setting 5 to 6 hours.

3. About 5 minutes before serving, remove pork from cooker; place on serving platter and cover to keep warm.

4. Mix water and cornstarch in 2-cup glass measuring cup or small microwavable bowl until smooth. Pour 1 cup of the juices from cooker into cornstarch mixture; mix well. Microwave uncovered on High 1 to 2 minutes, stirring once halfway through cooking, until mixture boils and thickens slightly. Serve sauce with pork.

Ingredient Substitution

If you happen to have bone-in chops in your freezer, you can use them in place of boneless chops—just make sure you thaw them in the refrigerator first.

Serving Suggestion

When it comes to side dishes to pair with this classic dish, think green and white. Steamed green beans or asparagus and creamy coleslaw make delicious accompaniments. Add some mashed potatoes and you'll have a family-pleasing meal.

1 Serving: Calories 240 (Calories from Fat 70); Fat 8g (Saturated 3g); Cholesterol 65mg; Sodium 510mg; Carbohydrate 19g (Dietary Fiber 1g); Protein 23g • **% Daily Value:** Vitamin A 2%; Vitamin C 2%; Calcium 2%; Iron 6% • **Diet Exchanges:** 1 Starch, 3 Lean Meat • **Carbohydrate Choices:** 1

Barbecued Pork Chops

Savory Barbecued Ribs

4 servings

SLOW COOKER:
4 1/2- to 6-quart

PREP TIME:
10 minutes

COOK TIME:
Low 8 to 9 hours

FINISHING COOK TIME:
Low 1 hour

3 1/2 pounds pork spareribs or loin back ribs

1/4 cup packed brown sugar

1/2 teaspoon hickory smoked salt

1/4 teaspoon pepper

1/2 cup cola

1 1/4 cups barbecue sauce

1. Spray inside of 4 1/2- to 6-quart slow cooker with cooking spray.

2. Trim excess fat and remove membranes from ribs. Mix brown sugar, hickory salt and pepper; rub mixture into ribs. Cut ribs into 2- or 3-rib portions. Place ribs in slow cooker; pour cola around ribs.

3. Cover and cook on low heat setting 8 to 9 hours or until ribs are tender.

4. Remove ribs from cooker; place in shallow baking pan. Drain liquid from cooker and discard. Brush both sides of ribs with barbecue sauce. Return ribs to cooker. Pour any remaining sauce over ribs. Cover and cook on low heat setting about 1 hour until ribs are glazed and sauce is desired consistency. Cut into single-rib servings if desired.

Betty's Success Tip

Hickory smoked salt adds a nice hint of barbecue flavor to these ribs. If you don't have smoky flavored salt on hand, use 1/2 teaspoon garlic salt instead.

Serving Suggestion

For a comforting homemade dinner, serve mashed potatoes and hot-from-the-oven corn bread. Don't forget to pass the butter to top off the potatoes and corn bread!

1 Serving: Calories 780 (Calories from Fat 425); Fat 47g (Saturated 17g); Cholesterol 185mg; Sodium 1100mg; Carbohydrate 44g (Dietary Fiber 0g); Protein 45g • **% Daily Value:** Vitamin A 4%; Vitamin C 2%; Calcium 10%; Iron 20% • **Diet Exchanges:** 3 Starch, 4 High-Fat Meat, 1 Fat • **Carbohydrate Choices:** 3

Savory Barbecued Ribs and Garlic-Parmesan Smashed Potatoes (page 204)

Honey-Dijon Ham

6 servings, with leftovers

SLOW COOKER:
4- to 6-quart

PREP TIME:
15 minutes

COOK TIME:
Low 6 to 8 hours

5-pound bone-in fully cooked smoked ham

1/3 cup apple juice

1/4 cup packed brown sugar

1 tablespoon honey

1 tablespoon Dijon mustard

Ingredient Substitution

Many types of mustard are delicious with ham. If you prefer the taste of country-style mustard, a coarsely ground mustard, or all-American yellow mustard, go ahead and use it—but then you may want to alter the name of the recipe as well!

Serving Suggestion

Baked potatoes and warm dinner rolls complete this family-friendly meal. Provide sour cream, chopped green onions, bacon bits and shredded cheese, and let everyone top their potatoes as they choose.

1. Place ham in 4- to 6-quart slow cooker. Add apple juice. Mix brown sugar, honey and mustard; spread over ham.

2. Cover and cook on low heat setting 6 to 8 hours or until ham is hot and glazed.

3. Remove ham from cooker; place on cutting board. Cut ham in half; reserve one half. Cut remaining half of ham into slices; place on serving platter to serve.

4. Cut reserved ham into 1/2-inch cubes. Place 1 1/2 cups cubes in each of 2 resealable plastic food-storage bags. Seal and label bags for Supper Ham Frittata (page 128) and Ham and Asparagus Chowder (page 129). Refrigerate both bags up to 3 days or freeze up to 1 month for later use. If frozen, thaw in refrigerator before using.

1 Serving: Calories 155 (Calories from Fat 45); Fat 5g (Saturated 2g); Cholesterol 50mg; Sodium 1130mg; Carbohydrate 8g (Dietary Fiber 0g); Protein 19g • **% Daily Value:** Vitamin A 0%; Vitamin C 0%; Calcium 0%; Iron 8% • **Diet Exchanges:** 1/2 Starch, 2 1/2 Lean Meat • **Carbohydrate Choices:** 1/2

Honey Dijon Ham and Candied Sweet Potatoes (page 155)

Supper Ham Frittata

4 servings

PREP TIME:
20 minutes

COOK TIME:
20 minutes

Betty's Success Tip

Don't let the word frittata throw you. A frittata is the Italian version of the American omelet. In a frittata, the ingredients are mixed in with the eggs instead of folded inside. Unlike omelets, frittatas are firm and round, because they're cooked slowly over low heat and not folded.

Serving Suggestion

This Italian-inspired egg dish makes a great weekend brunch. Serve with steamed fresh asparagus or broccoli spears, toasted English muffins and freshly squeezed orange juice.

1 1/2 cups frozen southern-style cubed hash brown potatoes (from 32-ounce bag)

1 medium zucchini, cut into fourths, then sliced (1 cup)

1 bag (1 1/2 cups) cubed cooked Honey-Dijon Ham (page 126) for Supper Ham Frittata, thawed if frozen

4 eggs

1/4 cup milk

1/4 teaspoon salt

1 cup shredded Cheddar cheese (4 ounces)

1. Spray 10-inch nonstick skillet with cooking spray; heat over medium-high heat. Cook potatoes, zucchini and ham in skillet 5 to 8 minutes, stirring frequently, until zucchini is crisp–tender and potatoes are thoroughly cooked.

2. Meanwhile, beat eggs in medium bowl. Add milk and salt; beat well.

3. Pour egg mixture over mixture in skillet; reduce heat to medium-low. Cover and cook 5 to 7 minutes, lifting edges occasionally to allow uncooked egg mixture to flow to bottom of skillet, until center is set.

4. Sprinkle cheese over frittata. Cover and cook 2 to 3 minutes or until cheese is melted. Cut into wedges.

➤ what a **Great Idea**...with Leftovers

1 Serving: Calories 330 (Calories from Fat 155); Fat 17g (Saturated 8g); Cholesterol 260mg; Sodium 830mg; Carbohydrate 21g (Dietary Fiber 1g); Protein 23g • **% Daily Value:** Vitamin A 16%; Vitamin C 6%; Calcium 20%; Iron 8% • **Diet Exchanges:** 1 1/2 Starch, 2 1/2 Lean Meat, 2 Fat • **Carbohydrate Choices:** 1 1/2

Ham and Asparagus Chowder

4 servings (1 1/3 cups each)

PREP TIME:
5 minutes

COOK TIME:
15 minutes

1 1/2 cups cubed unpeeled red potatoes

1/2 cup water

1 1/2 cups 1 1/2-inch pieces fresh asparagus

1 bag (1 1/2 cups) cubed cooked Honey-Dijon Ham (page 126)
    for Ham and Asparagus Chowder, thawed if frozen

1 can (10 3/4 ounces) condensed cream of mushroom soup

1 cup milk

Freshly ground black pepper, if desired

Ingredient Substitution

Fresh green asparagus mixed with pink ham makes this an elegant chowder to serve in springtime, when asparagus is at its peak. However, you can make this chowder with 1 1/2 cups of canned or thawed frozen whole kernel corn and enjoy it all year around.

1. Heat potatoes and water to boiling in 2-quart saucepan. Reduce heat to medium; cover and cook 5 minutes or until potatoes are crisp-tender.

2. Add asparagus and ham; cover and cook 3 to 5 minutes or until thoroughly heated. Stir in soup and milk. Heat over high heat, stirring occasionally, until hot. Sprinkle with pepper before serving.

Serving Suggestion

Mix up a package of corn muffin mix and pop them in the oven before preparing the chowder. Serve with honey to drizzle over the warm muffins.

➤ what a **Great Idea**...with Leftovers

1 Serving: Calories 260 (Calories from Fat 90); Fat 10g (Saturated 3g); Cholesterol 30mg; Sodium 1240mg; Carbohydrate 28g (Dietary Fiber 2g); Protein 15g • **% Daily Value:** Vitamin A 10%; Vitamin C 14%; Calcium 12%; Iron 10% • **Diet Exchanges:** 2 Starch, 1 Lean Meat, 1 Fat • **Carbohydrate Choices:** 2

5

Beans &Veggies

- Sweet Maple Baked Beans 132
- Southwestern Pinto Beans 133
- Country French White Beans 134
- Easy Savory Baked Beans 136
- Caribbean Black Beans 138
- New Orleans–Style Red Beans 139
- Barley Casserole with Peas and Peppers 140
- Spanish Rice with Tomatoes and Peppers 142
- Lentils and Veggies 144
- Sherry Buttered Mushrooms 145
- Southern-Style String Beans 146
- Orange-Glazed Beets 148
- Pineapple Carrots 149
- Cauliflower Curry 150
- The Ultimate Creamed Corn 152
- Greek-Style Veggies 153
- Sour Cream and Onion Potato Casserole 154
- Candied Sweet Potatoes 155
- Herbed Potatoes and Peppers 156

◀ Sweet Maple Baked Beans (page 132)

Sweet Maple Baked Beans

8 servings (1/2 cup each)

Photo on page 130

SLOW COOKER:
3 1/2- to 4-quart

PREP TIME:
2 hours

COOK TIME:
Low 8 to 10 hours

Betty's Success Tip

For the best flavor, use 100 percent pure maple syrup rather than a maple-flavored syrup. It may cost a little more, but it has much more flavor. Maple syrups are graded according to color and flavor; Grade B, a dark amber and hearty-flavored syrup, makes especially delicious baked beans.

Ingredient Substitution

In place of the onion, use 1 teaspoon onion powder or 1 tablespoon instant minced onion.

2 cups dried navy beans, sorted and rinsed

10 cups water

3/4 cup water

1 medium onion, chopped (1/2 cup)

3/4 cup real maple syrup

3 tablespoons packed brown sugar

2 teaspoons ground mustard

1/2 teaspoon ground ginger

1 teaspoon salt

1. Heat beans and 10 cups water to boiling in 6-quart Dutch oven; reduce heat. Cover and simmer 2 hours; drain.

2. Mix beans, 3/4 cup water and the remaining ingredients in 3 1/2- to 4-quart slow cooker.

3. Cover and cook on low heat setting 8 to 10 hours or until beans are very tender and most of the liquid has been absorbed.

1 Serving: Calories 310 (Calories from Fat 70); Fat 8g (Saturated 1g); Cholesterol 0mg; Sodium 300mg; Carbohydrate 57g (Dietary Fiber 8g); Protein 11g • **% Daily Value:** Vitamin A 0%; Vitamin C 0%; Calcium 10%; Iron 18% • **Diet Exchanges:** 3 Starch, 1 Fruit, 1/2 Fat • **Carbohydrate Choices:** 4

Southwestern Pinto Beans

7 servings (about 1/2 cup each)

SLOW COOKER:
3 1/2- to 4-quart

PREP TIME:
2 hours 15 minutes

COOK TIME:
Low 10 to 12 hours

FINISHING COOK TIME:
Low 15 to 30 minutes

Betty's Success Tip

Save the leftover chipotle chilies to add a fiery kick to salsa, tacos and other Mexican foods.

Serving Suggestion

You can vary the taste of this south-of-the-border-influenced side dish by using black beans instead of pinto beans. These Tex-Mex beans make a great side dish for grilled beef steak, pork chops or chicken.

4 cups water

1 cup dried pinto beans, sorted and rinsed

1 cup water

1 medium stalk celery, sliced (1/2 cup)

1 medium carrot, chopped (1/2 cup)

1 medium onion, chopped (1/2 cup)

2 cloves garlic, finely chopped

1 tablespoon chopped chipotle chilies in adobo sauce (from 7-ounce can)

1 teaspoon chili powder

1/2 teaspoon dried oregano leaves

2 teaspoons salt

1 can (6 ounces) tomato paste

1. Heat 4 cups water and the beans to boiling in 2-quart saucepan; reduce heat to low. Cover and simmer 2 hours.

2. Drain beans. Mix beans, 1 cup water and the remaining ingredients except salt and tomato paste in 3 1/2- to 4-quart slow cooker.

3. Cover and cook on low heat setting 10 to 12 hours or until beans are tender.

4. Stir in salt and tomato paste. Cover and cook on low heat setting 15 to 30 minutes or until thoroughly heated. If bean mixture becomes too thick, stir in up to 1/4 cup hot water, 1 tablespoon at a time, until desired consistency.

1 Serving: Calories 70 (Calories from Fat 0); Fat 0g (Saturated 0g); Cholesterol 0mg; Sodium 900mg; Carbohydrate 14g (Dietary Fiber 4g); Protein 3g • **% Daily Value:** Vitamin A 44%; Vitamin C 10%; Calcium 2%; Iron 6% • **Diet Exchanges:** 1 Starch • **Carbohydrate Choices:** 1

Country French White Beans

6 servings (1 cup each)

SLOW COOKER:
3 1/2- to 4-quart

SOAK:
10 hours

PREP TIME:
12 minutes

COOK TIME:
High 3 1/2 to 5 hours

Ingredient Substitution

Don't have any *herbes de Provence* on hand? Mix together 1 teaspoon dried thyme leaves, 1 teaspoon dried basil leaves, 1/2 teaspoon dried marjoram leaves and 1/2 teaspoon dried parsley flakes. Other herbs commonly used in *herbes de Provence* are fennel seed, lavender, rosemary and savory.

Serving Suggestion

This simple side dish will nicely complement herb-roasted chicken or roasted leg of lamb. Serve with a glass of red wine, and enjoy the flavors of France.

2 cups dried great northern beans, sorted and rinsed

1 large onion, chopped (1 cup)

2 cloves garlic, finely chopped

2 cups water

1 tablespoon dried herbes de Provence

3 tablespoons olive or vegetable oil

2 teaspoons salt

1/2 cup chopped drained roasted red bell peppers (from 7-ounce jar)

1. Place beans in large bowl. Add enough water to cover by 2 inches. Let soak overnight, at least 10 hours.

2. Drain beans. Mix beans and remaining ingredients except bell peppers in 3 1/2- to 4-quart slow cooker.

3. Cover and cook on high heat setting 3 hours 30 minutes to 5 hours or until beans are tender.

4. Stir bell peppers into beans in cooker.

1 Serving: Calories 250 (Calories from Fat 65); Fat 7g (Saturated 1g); Cholesterol 0mg; Sodium 800mg; Carbohydrate 42g (Dietary Fiber 10g); Protein 15g • **% Daily Value:** Vitamin A 18%; Vitamin C 22%; Calcium 14%; Iron 32% • **Diet Exchanges:** 2 Starch, 1 Very Lean Meat, 1 Fat • **Carbohydrate Choices:** 3

Country French White Beans

Easy Savory Baked Beans

18 servings (1/2 cup each)

SLOW COOKER:
3 1/2- to 4-quart

PREP TIME:
15 minutes

COOK TIME:
High 1 hour; Low 5 to 7 hours

Betty's Success Tip

The baked bean pot is the fore-runner of the slow cooker. The very first slow cookers were simple bean cookers and were even referred to as "beaneries."

Serving Suggestion

Spoon the beans over squares of hot corn bread or split corn bread muffins. Sprinkle with shredded Cheddar cheese and sliced green onion.

1/2 pound bacon, cut into 1/2-inch pieces

1/2 cup packed brown sugar

1/4 cup cornstarch

1 teaspoon ground mustard

1/2 cup molasses

1 tablespoon white vinegar

4 cans (16 ounces each) baked beans

1 medium green bell pepper, chopped (1 cup)

1 medium onion, chopped (1/2 cup)

1. Cook bacon in 10-inch skillet over medium heat, stirring occasionally, until crisp. Drain, reserving 2 tablespoons drippings.

2. Mix cooked bacon, 2 tablespoons drippings and remaining ingredients in 3 1/2- to 4-quart slow cooker.

3. Cover and cook on high heat setting 1 hour.

4. Turn to low heat setting; cook 5 to 7 hours to blend and develop flavors.

1 Serving: Calories 185 (Calories from Fat 25); Fat 3g (Saturated 1g); Cholesterol 10mg; Sodium 510mg; Carbohydrate 34g (Dietary Fiber 5g); Protein 6g • **% Daily Value:** Vitamin A 18%; Vitamin C 8%; Calcium 8%; Iron 22% • **Diet Exchanges:** 2 Starch, 1/2 Fat • **Carbohydrate Choices:** 1 1/2

Celebrate Summer

Toss your favorite slow cooker meal together in the morning and let it simmer all day long for a fun summer get-together. With no stove to turn on, you—and your kitchen—stay cool as cucumbers. Celebrate summer slow-cooker style with some of these great picks for fun summer get-togethers:

Event	Appetizers, Snacks or Sides	Beef	Chicken	Ham/Pork
Backyard Barbecue or Picnic	Sweet Maple Baked Beans (page 132)	Barbecued Beef and Pork Sandwiches (page 163)	Teriyaki Barbecued Chicken Sandwiches (page 160)	Ham with Cheesy Potatoes (page 88)
Father's Day	Garlic-Parmesan Smashed Potatoes (page 204)	Beef Roast with Shiitake Mushroom Sauce (page 102)	Chicken Stew (page 68)	Barbecued Pork Chops (page 122)
Fourth of July	Hot and Spicy Riblets (page 31)	Beef au Jus Sandwiches (page 166)	Chicken-Wild Rice Casserole with Dried Cherries (page 69)	Ham with Fruit Chutney (page 87)
Graduation Party	Spiced Party Nut Mix (page 35)	Mini Cheeseburger Bites (page 26)	White Chili with Chicken (page 61)	Southwestern Pork Burritos (page 168)
Memorial Day Party	Easy Savory Baked Beans (page 136)	Crowd-Pleasing Chili (page 172)	Chicken and Sausage Jambalaya (page 174)	Smoky Ham and Navy Bean Stew (page 49)
Pool Party	Party Crab Dip (page 16)	Asian Meatballs (page 178)	Chicken and Bean Tacos (page 162)	Savory Barbecued Ribs (page 124)

To Market, To Market

There's nothing like peak-of-season freshness for the best taste in your favorite recipes:

Vegetable	Peak	Recipe
Asparagus	Mar.-July	Beef and Asparagus Over Noodles (page 104); Ham and Asparagus Chowder (page 129)
Avocados	June	Make-Your-Own Taco Salad (page 176)
Beans (Green)	May-Nov.	Southern-Style String Beans (page 146)
Leeks	Sept.-Nov.	Fisherman's Wharf Seafood Stew (page 52)
Onions (Walla Walla)	June-Aug.	Corned Beef Brisket with Horseradish Sour Cream (page 79)
Potatoes (Red)	Aug.-Jan.	Beef Carbonnade with Potatoes (page 76); Beef Pot Roast with Vegetables (page 78); Corned Beef and Cabbage Dinner (page 108); Creamed Potatoes with Garden Peas (page 206); Curried Pork Stew (page 58); Ham and Asparagus Chowder (page 129); Savory Beef Short Rib Dinner (page 112)
Spinach	Jan.-July	Black-Eyed Pea and Sausage Soup (page 48); Chicken and Vegetable Tortellini Stew (page 50)
Squash (Butternut)	Aug.-Mar.	Honey-Cranberry Butternut Squash (page 210)

Caribbean Black Beans

8 servings (1/2 cup each)

SLOW COOKER:
3 1/2- to 4-quart

PREP TIME:
10 minutes

COOK TIME:
Low 5 to 6 hours

Betty's Success Tip

You're probably most familiar with pimientos as a stuffing in green olives. Pimientos can be purchased canned or bottled. They taste sweeter and more succulent than red bell peppers.

Serving Suggestion

This black bean dish tastes great as a meatless main dish with rice. Place a mound of hot rice in the middle of each individual shallow bowl and spoon the black bean mixture around the rice. Serve with plenty of chopped red onion and hard-cooked eggs to sprinkle on top.

2 cans (15 ounces each) black beans, rinsed and drained

1/2 cup water

1 medium green bell pepper, chopped (1 cup)

1 medium onion, chopped (1/2 cup)

1 teaspoon ground cumin

1/2 teaspoon salt

1/2 teaspoon garlic powder

1 jar (2 ounces) diced pimientos, drained

1. Mix all ingredients in 3 1/2- to 4-quart slow cooker.

2. Cover and cook on low heat setting 5 to 6 hours to blend and develop flavors.

1 Serving: Calories 140 (Calories from Fat 10); Fat 1g (Saturated 0g); Cholesterol 0mg; Sodium 560mg; Carbohydrate 30g (Dietary Fiber 7g); Protein 10g • **% Daily Value:** Vitamin A 4%; Vitamin C 16%; Calcium 8%; Iron 16% • **Diet Exchanges:** 2 Starch • **Carbohydrate Choices:** 2

New Orleans–Style Red Beans

8 servings (1/2 cup each)

SLOW COOKER:
3 1/2- to 4-quart

PREP TIME:
10 minutes

COOK TIME:
Low 4 to 6 hours

Betty's Success Tip

If you enjoy a bit of heat, shake in some red pepper sauce during the last hour of cooking, but not before, since hot sauce will become stronger-tasting and bitter over long, slow cooking. You can also pass a bottle of red pepper sauce at the table so everyone can season the beans as desired.

Serving Suggestion

Pair these savory beans with spicy andouille sausage or shrimp hot off the grill, heaping spoonfuls of hot rice and a side of fried okra for a southern-style dinner experience.

1/4 cup sliced celery

2 cans (15 1/2 ounces each) red kidney beans, drained

1 small green bell pepper, chopped (1/2 cup)

1 medium onion, chopped (1/2 cup)

2 cloves garlic, finely chopped

1 teaspoon dried thyme leaves

1/2 teaspoon salt

1/4 teaspoon crushed red pepper flakes

1 can (8 ounces) tomato sauce

Red pepper sauce, if desired

1. Place celery in 3 1/2- to 4-quart slow cooker. Layer remaining ingredients except pepper sauce over celery.

2. Cover and cook on low heat setting 4 to 6 hours or until desired consistency. Serve with pepper sauce.

1 Serving: Calories 135 (Calories from Fat 10); Fat 1g (Saturated 0g); Cholesterol 0mg; Sodium 600mg; Carbohydrate 29g (Dietary Fiber 8g); Protein 10g • **% Daily Value:** Vitamin A 4%; Vitamin C 12%; Calcium 4%; Iron 20% • **Diet Exchanges:** 1 1/2 Starch, 1 Vegetable • **Carbohydrate Choices:** 2

Barley Casserole with Peas and Peppers

9 servings (1/2 cup each)

SLOW COOKER:
3 1/2- to 4-quart

PREP TIME:
10 minutes

COOK TIME:
Low 5 to 6 hours

FINISHING COOK TIME:
High 15 to 20 minutes

Betty's Success Tip

Did you know? One cup of barley provides the same amount of protein as an 8-ounce glass of milk.

Ingredient Substitution

If you're trying to lower your sodium intake, use reduced-sodium chicken broth instead of the regular variety.

1 cup uncooked barley

1/2 cup water

2 tablespoons butter or margarine, melted

3/4 teaspoon seasoned salt

1/2 teaspoon dried thyme leaves

1/4 teaspoon pepper

1 medium onion, chopped (1/2 cup)

1 can (14 ounces) chicken broth

1 cup frozen green peas (from 1-pound bag)

1/4 cup finely chopped drained roasted red bell peppers
    (from 7-ounce jar)

1. Mix all ingredients except peas and bell peppers in 3 1/2- to 4-quart slow cooker.

2. Cover and cook on low heat setting 5 to 6 hours or until barley is tender.

3. Stir in peas and bell peppers. Cover and cook on high heat setting 15 to 20 minutes or until hot.

1 Serving: Calories 125 (Calories from Fat 25); Fat 3g (Saturated 2g); Cholesterol 5mg; Sodium 340mg; Carbohydrate 21g (Dietary Fiber 5g); Protein 4g • **% Daily Value:** Vitamin A 10%; Vitamin C 8%; Calcium 2%; Iron 4% • **Diet Exchanges:** 1 Starch, 1 Vegetable, 1/2 Fat • **Carbohydrate Choices:** 1 1/2

Barley Casserole with Peas and Peppers

Spanish Rice with Tomatoes and Peppers

10 servings (1/2 cup each)

SLOW COOKER:
3 1/2- to 4-quart

PREP TIME:
8 minutes

COOK TIME:
Low 2 to 3 hours

Ingredient Substitution

Use 1/8 teaspoon garlic powder or 1/4 teaspoon instant minced garlic in place of the fresh garlic, if needed.

Finishing Touch

This scrumptious side dish makes a great filling for burritos. Top with a dollop of sour cream, and garnish with a lime wedge or avocado slice before serving.

1 cup uncooked regular long-grain rice

1 cup water

1 medium onion, chopped (1/2 cup)

1 small green bell pepper, chopped (1/2 cup)

1 clove garlic, finely chopped

1 teaspoon chili powder

1 teaspoon ground cumin

1/2 teaspoon salt

1 can (14 1/2 ounces) diced tomatoes, undrained

1. Spray 3 1/2- to 4-quart slow cooker with cooking spray. Mix all ingredients except tomatoes in cooker. Top with tomatoes.

2. Cover and cook on low heat setting 2 to 3 hours or until rice and vegetables are tender and most of the liquid has been absorbed.

1 Serving: Calories 85 (Calories from Fat 0); Fat 0g (Saturated 0g); Cholesterol 0mg; Sodium 180mg; Carbohydrate 19g (Dietary Fiber 1g); Protein 2g • **% Daily Value:** Vitamin A 4%; Vitamin C 10%; Calcium 2%; Iron 6% • **Diet Exchanges:** 1 Starch • **Carbohydrate Choices:** 1

Spanish Rice with Tomatoes and Peppers

Lentils and Veggies

8 servings (1/2 cup each)

SLOW COOKER:
3 1/2- to 4-quart

PREP TIME:
15 minutes

COOK TIME:
Low 4 to 6 hours

Betty's Success Tip

A popular ingredient in the Middle East and India, lentils are a good source of iron and phosphorus. Leftover cooked lentils can be frozen in an airtight container for up to 2 months. Then reheat, covered, in a microwavable container until warm.

Finishing Touch

This lentil dish is extra delicious when topped with yogurt and shredded coconut to give it an Indian spin. You may also want to stir in a little ground red pepper before adding the toppings.

1 cup dried lentils (8 ounces), sorted and rinsed

2 medium carrots, sliced (1 cup)

1 medium onion, chopped (1/2 cup)

2 cloves garlic, finely chopped

1 teaspoon dried thyme leaves

1/4 teaspoon pepper

2 1/2 cups water

1 can (14 1/2 ounces) diced tomatoes, undrained

1 teaspoon salt

1. Mix all ingredients except tomatoes and salt in 3 1/2- to 4-quart slow cooker.

2. Cover and cook on low heat setting 4 to 6 hours or until lentils are tender.

3. Stir in tomatoes and salt.

1 Serving: Calories 75 (Calories from Fat 0); Fat 0g (Saturated 0g); Cholesterol 0mg; Sodium 380mg; Carbohydrate 18g (Dietary Fiber 6g); Protein 7g • **% Daily Value:** Vitamin A 32%; Vitamin C 8%; Calcium 2%; Iron 14% • **Diet Exchanges:** 1/2 Starch, 2 Vegetable • **Carbohydrate Choices:** 1

Sherry Buttered Mushrooms

25 servings (3 mushrooms each)

SLOW COOKER:
3 1/2- to 4-quart

PREP TIME:
15 minutes

COOK TIME:
High 2 hours

HOLD TIME:
High up to 2 hours

Betty's Success Tip

These buttery mushrooms are the perfect accompaniment for beef. Serve them with an herbed roast or with grilled steaks. Or use them to dress up grilled hamburger patties.

Ingredient Substitution

If you prefer not to use sherry, substitute 3 tablespoons balsamic vinegar or apple juice or cider instead.

1/2 cup butter or margarine, melted

1 teaspoon beef base or beef bouillon granules

2 tablespoons chopped fresh chives

2 cloves garlic, finely chopped

3 tablespoons dry sherry

2 pounds fresh whole mushrooms

1. Mix butter and beef base in 3 1/2- to 4-quart slow cooker. Add remaining ingredients; stir gently to coat mushrooms.

2. Cover and cook on high heat setting about 2 hours or until hot. Gently stir.

3. Serve with slotted spoon. Appetizers will hold on high heat setting up to 2 hours.

3 Mushrooms: Calories 50 (Calories from Fat 35); Fat 4g (Saturated 2g); Cholesterol 10mg; Sodium 75mg; Carbohydrate 2g (Dietary Fiber 0g); Protein 1g • **% Daily Value:** Vitamin A 2%; Vitamin C 0%; Calcium 0%; Iron 2% • **Diet Exchanges:** 1 Fat • **Carbohydrate Choices:** 0

Southern-Style String Beans

10 servings (1/2 cup each)

SLOW COOKER:
3 1/2- to 4-quart

PREP TIME:
10 minutes

COOK TIME:
Low 6 to 8 hours

1/2 pound boneless smoked ham or pork chops, cubed

1 1/2 pounds fresh green beans, cut into 1- to 2-inch pieces

1 medium onion, cut into eighths

1 cup water

1 teaspoon salt

1/4 teaspoon pepper

Betty's Success Tip

Southern "string" beans are traditionally simmered in a ham broth made with a ham bone or ham hock until tender and very flavorful. They're considered a real treat in the South. This recipe uses smoked ham or pork chops because they're easier to find.

Serving Suggestion

Serve this summertime southern side dish with fried chicken, fresh lemonade and coconut layer cake. It's like having a picnic at your dining room table.

1. Mix all ingredients in 3 1/2- to 4-quart slow cooker.

2. Cover and cook on low heat setting 6 to 8 hours or until beans are tender.

1 Serving: Calories 60 (Calories from Fat 20); Fat 2g (Saturated 1g); Cholesterol 10mg; Sodium 530mg; Carbohydrate 5g (Dietary Fiber 2g); Protein 5g • **% Daily Value:** Vitamin A 6%; Vitamin C 2%; Calcium 2%; Iron 4% • **Diet Exchanges:** 1/2 Medium-Fat Meat, 1 Vegetable • **Carbohydrate Choices:** 0

Southern-Style String Beans

Orange-Glazed Beets

6 servings (1/2 cup each)

SLOW COOKER:
3 1/2- to 4-quart

PREP TIME:
20 minutes

COOK TIME:
Low 11 to 12 hours

FINISHING COOK TIME:
High 5 to 10 minutes

2 pounds beets, peeled and cut into 1/2-inch slices (3 cups)

1/2 cup orange juice

1/4 cup cider vinegar

3 tablespoons honey

1 teaspoon salt

1 tablespoon cornstarch

1 tablespoon cold water

1. Mix all ingredients except cornstarch and water in 3 1/2- to 4-quart slow cooker.

2. Cover and cook on low heat setting 11 to 12 hours or until beets are tender.

3. Mix cornstarch and water; stir into beets. Cook uncovered on high heat setting 5 to 10 minutes or until sauce has thickened.

Betty's Success Tip

These sweet-and-sour beets are also referred to as Harvard beets. If you find beets with crisp, bright greens still attached, buy them because they'll be very fresh. Just make sure to remove the greens as soon as you get them home since they pull moisture from the beets.

Ingredient Substitution

In place of the cornstarch, use 2 tablespoons all-purpose flour or 4 teaspoons quick-cooking tapioca.

1 Serving: Calories 95 (Calories from Fat 0); Fat 0g (Saturated 0g); Cholesterol 0mg; Sodium 470mg; Carbohydrate 22g (Dietary Fiber 2g); Protein 2g • **% Daily Value:** Vitamin A 0%; Vitamin C 8%; Calcium 2%; Iron 4% • **Diet Exchanges:** 1 Starch, 1/2 Fruit • **Carbohydrate Choices:** 1 1/2

Pineapple Carrots

6 servings (1/2 cup each)

SLOW COOKER:
3 1/2- to 4-quart

PREP TIME:
10 minutes

COOK TIME:
High 4 to 5 hours

Betty's Success Tip

These bite-size, super-sweet carrots taste so good, your kids won't even realize what they're eating!

Serving Suggestion

The pineapple in this sweet side dish tastes wonderful when served with a ham main meal. Try pairing Pineapple Carrots with Ham with Fruit Chutney (page 87) or Honey-Dijon Ham (page 126).

1 bag (16 ounces) baby-cut carrots

1 can (8 ounces) pineapple tidbits in juice, undrained

2 tablespoons packed brown sugar

2 tablespoons butter or margarine, melted

2 teaspoons grated orange peel

1/2 teaspoon salt

1/2 teaspoon ground cinnamon

1/4 teaspoon ground nutmeg

1. Place carrots and pineapple in 3 1/2- to 4-quart slow cooker. Mix remaining ingredients; pour over carrots and pineapple.

2. Cover and cook on high heat setting 4 to 5 hours or until carrots are tender.

1 Serving: Calories 110 (Calories from Fat 35); Fat 4g (Saturated 2g); Cholesterol 10mg; Sodium 250mg; Carbohydrate 18g (Dietary Fiber 3g); Protein 1g • **% Daily Value:** Vitamin A 100%; Vitamin C 8%; Calcium 4%; Iron 4% • **Diet Exchanges:** 1 Fruit, 1 Fat • **Carbohydrate Choices:** 1

Cauliflower Curry

13 servings (1/2 cup each)

SLOW COOKER:
3 1/2- to 4-quart

PREP TIME:
15 minutes

COOK TIME:
Low 4 to 6 hours

FINISHING COOK TIME:
Low 10 to 15 minutes

Betty's Success Tip

You may want to remove the skins of the tomatoes when making this dish. To do so, dip the tomato in boiling water for 1 minute, make a slit in the skin and slowly peel it off.

Finishing Touch

Serve small bowls of traditional curry dish toppers such as toasted shredded coconut, chopped peanuts and raisins. The saltiness of the peanuts and the sweetness of the coconut and raisins enhance the flavor of the curry powder.

4 cups cauliflowerets

3 medium tomatoes, seeded and coarsely chopped (2 1/4 cups)

1 medium onion, chopped (1/2 cup)

1 can (14 ounces) coconut milk (not cream of coconut)

1 tablespoon soy sauce

1 1/2 teaspoons curry powder

1/2 teaspoon salt

1/2 teaspoon dried basil leaves

6 ounces baby spinach leaves

1. Mix cauliflowerets, tomatoes and onion in 3 1/2- to 4-quart slow cooker. Mix remaining ingredients except spinach; pour over vegetables.

2. Cover and cook on low heat setting 4 to 6 hours or until cauliflowerets are tender.

3. Stir in spinach leaves. Cover and cook on low heat setting 10 to 15 minutes or until spinach is tender. Spoon into small bowls to serve.

1 Serving: Calories 90 (Calories from Fat 55); Fat 6g (Saturated 5g); Cholesterol 0mg; Sodium 200mg; Carbohydrate 7g (Dietary Fiber 2g); Protein 2g • **% Daily Value:** Vitamin A 28%; Vitamin C 20%; Calcium 2%; Iron 4% • **Diet Exchanges:** 1 1/2 Vegetable, 1 Fat • **Carbohydrate Choices:** 1/2

Cauliflower Curry

The Ultimate Creamed Corn

5 servings (about 1/2 cup each)

SLOW COOKER:
3 1/2- to 4-quart

PREP TIME:
8 minutes

COOK TIME:
High 2 to 3 hours

Betty's Success Tip

Patience is a virtue! Resist the urge to peek inside the slow cooker during the cooking process. Every time you lift the lid, you add 15 to 20 minutes to the cooking time.

Finishing Touch

To add crunch, sprinkle crushed crackers or corn chips over the top of this delicious, creamy side dish.

1 bag (1 pound) frozen whole kernel corn

2 packages (3 ounces each) cream cheese, cut into cubes

1/2 cup milk

1/4 cup butter or margarine, melted

1 teaspoon sugar

1/2 teaspoon salt

1/8 teaspoon pepper

1. Spread corn over bottom of 3 1/2- to 4-quart slow cooker. Top with cream cheese cubes. Mix remaining ingredients; pour over corn and cream cheese.

2. Cover and cook on high heat setting 2 to 3 hours or until creamy. Stir well before serving.

1 Serving: Calories 300 (Calories from Fat 200); Fat 22g (Saturated 14g); Cholesterol 65mg; Sodium 410mg; Carbohydrate 20g (Dietary Fiber 2g); Protein 6g • **% Daily Value:** Vitamin A 20%; Vitamin C 2%; Calcium 6%; Iron 4% • **Diet Exchanges:** 1 Starch, 1 Vegetable, 4 Fat • **Carbohydrate Choices:** 1

Greek-Style Veggies

16 servings (1/2 cup each)

SLOW COOKER:
3 1/2- to 4-quart

PREP TIME:
20 minutes

COOK TIME:
Low 7 to 8 hours

Betty's Success Tip

You'll find many of the ingredients for this dish, such as zucchini, eggplant, red bell pepper, onions and mushrooms, at your local farmers' market.

Serving Suggestion

Make this vegetable-filled side dish a meal by serving over cooked rice or noodles. Warmed pita slices, followed by baklava for dessert, play up the Greek theme.

2 medium zucchini, cut into 1/2-inch slices (4 cups)

1 medium eggplant, peeled and cut into 1/2-inch cubes (4 cups)

1 medium red bell pepper, cut into strips

1 medium onion, chopped (1/2 cup)

1 package (8 ounces) whole mushrooms, cut into fourths

3 cloves garlic, finely chopped

1 can (28 ounces) tomato puree, undrained

1 can (2 1/4 ounces) sliced ripe olives, drained

2 teaspoons salt

2 teaspoons dried basil leaves

1/2 teaspoon dried thyme leaves

1/4 teaspoon pepper

1 cup crumbled feta cheese, if desired

1. Mix all ingredients except cheese in 3 1/2- to 4-quart slow cooker.

2. Cover and cook on low heat setting 7 to 8 hours or until vegetables are tender.

3. Top each serving with 1 tablespoon cheese.

1 Serving: Calories 60 (Calories from Fat 10); Fat 1g (Saturated 0g); Cholesterol 0mg; Sodium 530mg; Carbohydrate 10g (Dietary Fiber 3g); Protein 2g • **% Daily Value:** Vitamin A 20%; Vitamin C 18%; Calcium 2%; Iron 6% • **Diet Exchanges:** 2 Vegetable • **Carbohydrate Choices:** 1/2

Sour Cream and Onion
Potato Casserole

24 servings (1/2 cup each)

SLOW COOKER:
3 1/2- to 4-quart

PREP TIME:
5 minutes

COOK TIME:
Low 5 to 6 hours

HOLD TIME:
Low up to 2 hours

Betty's Success Tip

Make sure you use melted butter or margarine in this recipe, because solid butter or margarine will not coat the hash browns as evenly.

Ingredient Substitution

Can't find chive and onion sour cream potato topper at your supermarket? Make your own by adding 1/2 cup chopped fresh or 3 tablespoons dried chives and 1 teaspoon onion salt to three 8-ounce containers of sour cream.

3 packages (5.2 ounces each) hash brown potato mix

3 tablespoons butter or margarine, melted

5 cups water

1 can (10 3/4 ounces) condensed cream of mushroom soup

2 containers (12 ounces each) chive and onion sour cream potato topper

2 cups shredded Cheddar and American cheese blend (8 ounces)

1/2 cup French-fried onions (from 2.8-ounce can)

1. Toss potatoes (dry) and butter in 3 1/2- to 4-quart slow cooker. Stir in water, soup, potato topper and cheese.

2. Cover and cook on low heat setting 5 to 6 hours or until liquid is absorbed.

3. To serve, sprinkle onions on top. Potatoes will hold on low heat setting up to 2 hours.

1 Serving: Calories 140 (Calories from Fat 90); Fat 10g (Saturated 6g); Cholesterol 25mg; Sodium 410mg; Carbohydrate 8g (Dietary Fiber 1g); Protein 4g • **% Daily Value:** Vitamin A 6%; Vitamin C 0%; Calcium 8%; Iron 0% • **Diet Exchanges:** 1/2 Starch, 1/2 High-Fat Meat, 1 Fat • **Carbohydrate Choices:** 1/2

Candied Sweet Potatoes

12 servings (about 1/2 cup each)

Photo on page 127

SLOW COOKER:
3 1/2- to 4-quart

PREP TIME:
35 minutes

COOK TIME:
Low 6 to 8 hours

FINISHING COOK TIME:
Low 10 minutes

Betty's Success Tip

Many varieties of sweet potatoes are sold in supermarkets. The sweet potatoes with darker skin (often labeled "yams") not only make a richer-colored dish, but also a tastier, sweeter one. The very light-colored sweet potatoes are not as sweet and are often drier.

Serving Suggestion

Put the emphasis on candied and marshmallow when passing this dish around the Thanksgiving table, and kids will have a hard time not trying a bite. Serve with turkey, cranberry sauce, mashed potatoes and gravy.

4 pounds dark-orange sweet potatoes (about 10), peeled and cut into 1-inch cubes

3/4 cup butter or margarine

2 cups packed brown sugar

1/2 cup orange juice

1 tablespoon ground cinnamon

2 teaspoons grated lemon peel

2 teaspoons salt

1/2 teaspoon ground nutmeg

2 cups miniature marshmallows or 25 large marshmallows

1. Place sweet potatoes in 3 1/2- to 4-quart slow cooker.

2. Place butter in medium microwavable bowl. Microwave uncovered on High about 1 minute or until melted. Stir in remaining ingredients except marshmallows; pour over sweet potatoes. Stir to coat sweet potatoes with butter mixture.

3. Cover and cook on low heat setting 6 to 8 hours or until potatoes are very tender.

4. Sprinkle marshmallows over potatoes. Cover and cook on low heat setting about 10 minutes or until marshmallows are melted. Serve with a slotted spoon.

1 Serving: Calories 405 (Calories from Fat 110); Fat 12g (Saturated 7g); Cholesterol 30mg; Sodium 500mg; Carbohydrate 72g (Dietary Fiber 4g); Protein 2g • **% Daily Value:** Vitamin A 100%; Vitamin C 26%; Calcium 8%; Iron 8% • **Diet Exchanges:** 1 Starch, 4 Fruit, 2 Fat • **Carbohydrate Choices:** 5

Herbed Potatoes and Peppers

14 servings (1/2 cup each)

SLOW COOKER:
3 1/2- to 4-quart

PREP TIME:
15 minutes

COOK TIME:
High 4 to 6 hours

Serving Suggestion

Refrigerate the leftovers, and serve them the next day as a delicious potato salad. Tangy and tomato-ey, it makes a nice change from the usual mayonnaise-based potato salad and it's delicious with grilled chicken breast, hamburger patties or pork chops.

Finishing Touch

If you like your bell peppers with a bit of crunch, add them to the mixture during the last 15 minutes of cooking.

2 pounds small red potatoes, cut into eighths

1 medium green bell pepper, cut into strips

1 medium red bell pepper, cut into strips

2 cloves garlic, finely chopped

1/2 cup water

1 1/2 teaspoons salt

1 teaspoon dried basil leaves

1 teaspoon dried oregano leaves

1 can (14 1/2 ounces) diced tomatoes, undrained

Shredded Parmesan cheese, if desired

1. Place potatoes in 3 1/2- to 4-quart slow cooker.

2. Layer bell peppers and garlic over potatoes. Pour water into cooker. Top with remaining ingredients except cheese, adding tomatoes last.

3. Cover and cook on high heat setting 4 to 6 hours or until potatoes are tender. Serve with cheese.

1 Serving: Calories 70 (Calories from Fat 0); Fat 0g (Saturated 0g); Cholesterol 0mg; Sodium 300mg; Carbohydrate 16g (Dietary Fiber 2g); Protein 2g • **% Daily Value:** Vitamin A 12%; Vitamin C 28%; Calcium 2%; Iron 4% • **Diet Exchanges:** 1 Starch • **Carbohydrate Choices:** 1

Herbed Potatoes and Peppers

Make It
& Take It

6

- Teriyaki Barbecued Chicken Sandwiches 160
- Chicken and Bean Tacos 162
- Barbecued Beef and Pork Sandwiches 163
- Beef au Jus Sandwiches 166
- Southwestern Pork Burritos 168
- Pizza Joe Sandwiches 170
- Turkey Chili 171
- Crowd-Pleasing Chili 172
- Hamburger Hash 173
- Chicken and Sausage Jambalaya 174
- Make-Your-Own Taco Salad 176
- Beef and Green Chile Tortilla Dinner 177
- Asian Meatballs 178
- Swedish Meatballs 180
- Texas-Style Barbecued Beans 181
- Southwestern Calico Baked Beans 182
- Baked Potato Bar 183
- Cheesy Ravioli Casserole 184

Turkey Chili (page 171)

Teriyaki Barbecued Chicken Sandwiches

10 sandwiches

SLOW COOKER:
3 1/2- to 4-quart

PREP TIME:
10 minutes

COOK TIME:
Low 6 to 7 hours

HOLD TIME:
Low up to 2 hours

2 packages (20 ounces each) boneless, skinless chicken thighs (about 24 thighs)

1 envelope (1 ounce) stir-fry seasoning mix

1/2 cup ketchup

1/4 cup stir-fry sauce

2 1/2 cups coleslaw mix

10 kaiser rolls

Betty's Success Tip

Stir-fry sauces are available in many varieties, from salty to sweet and mild to hot and spicy. Look for them in the Asian-foods section of your supermarket. The sauces are usually made from soy sauce, sesame oil, garlic and various spices.

Ingredient Substitution

Up the flavor factor by replacing the regular ketchup with one of the new hot and spicy or mesquite-flavored ketchups currently available.

1. Place chicken in 3 1/2- to 4-quart slow cooker. Mix seasoning mix (dry), ketchup and stir-fry sauce; pour over chicken.

2. Cover and cook on low heat setting 6 to 7 hours or until juice of chicken is no longer pink when centers of thickest pieces are cut and chicken is tender.

3. Pull chicken into shreds, using 2 forks. Stir well to mix chicken with sauce. To serve, place 1/4 cup coleslaw mix on roll and top with chicken. Chicken mixture will hold on low heat setting up to 2 hours.

1 Sandwich: Calories 365 (Calories from Fat 110); Fat 12g (Saturated 3g); Cholesterol 70mg; Sodium 760mg; Carbohydrate 34g (Dietary Fiber 3g); Protein 30g • **% Daily Value:** Vitamin A 4%; Vitamin C 14%; Calcium 10%; Iron 26% • **Diet Exchanges:** 2 Starch, 3 Lean Meat, 1 Vegetable • **Carbohydrate Choices:** 1 1/2

Teriyaki Barbecued Chicken Sandwiches

Chicken and Bean Tacos

24 tacos

SLOW COOKER:
3 1/2- to 4-quart

PREP TIME:
10 minutes

COOK TIME:
Low 7 to 8 hours

HOLD TIME:
Low up to 3 hours

Ingredient Substitution

Cannellini beans are large white kidney beans. Feel free to substitute any kind of bean in this recipe. Use your favorite, or try great northern, lima, butter or pinto beans.

Serving Suggestion

Instead of using taco shells, take a bag of tortilla or corn chips to the party. Everyone can spoon the spicy shredded chicken over the chips and add their own toppings.

1 1/4 pounds boneless, skinless chicken thighs (about 6 thighs)

3 tablespoons taco seasoning mix (from 1 1/4-ounce envelope)

1 can (4 1/2 ounces) chopped green chiles, undrained

1 can (8 ounces) tomato sauce

1 teaspoon ground cumin

1 teaspoon coriander seed, crushed

1 can (19 ounces) cannellini beans, drained

2 packages (4.6 ounces each) taco shells (12 shells each)

1 1/2 cups shredded Cheddar cheese (6 ounces)

1 1/2 cups shredded lettuce

1 container (8 ounces) sour cream (1 cup)

1 cup thick-and-chunky salsa

1. Place chicken in 3 1/2- to 4-quart slow cooker. Sprinkle with taco seasoning mix; top with chiles. Mix tomato sauce, cumin and coriander seed in medium bowl; pour over chicken. Top with beans.

2. Cover and cook on low heat setting 7 to 8 hours or until juice of chicken is no longer pink when centers of thickest pieces are cut and chicken is tender.

3. Remove chicken from cooker; place on cutting board. Mash beans in cooker. Shred chicken with 2 forks; return to cooker and mix well.

4. Serve chicken mixture with taco shells, cheese, lettuce, sour cream and salsa. Chicken mixture will hold on low heat setting up to 3 hours.

1 Taco: Calories 185 (Calories from Fat 80); Fat 9g (Saturated 4g); Cholesterol 30mg; Sodium 290mg; Carbohydrate 16g (Dietary Fiber 3g); Protein 10g • **% Daily Value:** Vitamin A 10%; Vitamin C 4%; Calcium 10%; Iron 10% • **Diet Exchanges:** 1 Starch, 1 Medium-Fat Meat, 1 Fat • **Carbohydrate Choices:** 1

Barbecued Beef and Pork Sandwiches

12 sandwiches

SLOW COOKER:
3 1/2- to 4-quart

PREP TIME:
15 minutes

COOK TIME:
Low 8 to 10 hours

FINISHING COOK TIME:
High 5 to 10 minutes

HOLD TIME:
Low up to 2 hours

Ingredient Substitution

Cooking beef and pork together adds to the unique flavor of these barbecued sandwiches. But if you prefer, this recipe may also be prepared using all beef or all pork.

Serving Suggestion

You can use whatever bread you like for these hearty sandwiches. Italian bread, hot dog buns and pita bread all make a nice change from hamburger buns. For an added twist, top each sandwich with a slice of Cheddar or Monterey Jack cheese.

1 1/2-pound beef boneless chuck or arm roast, trimmed of fat and cut into 2-inch pieces

1 1/2-pound pork boneless loin or shoulder roast, trimmed of fat and cut into 3-inch pieces

3 medium onions, chopped (1 1/2 cups)

1 medium green bell pepper, chopped (1 cup)

1/2 cup packed brown sugar

1/4 cup white vinegar

3 teaspoons chili powder

1 teaspoon salt

1 teaspoon ground mustard

2 teaspoons Worcestershire sauce

1 can (6 ounces) tomato paste

12 sandwich buns, split

1. Mix all ingredients except tomato paste and buns in 3 1/2- to 4-quart slow cooker.

2. Cover and cook on low heat setting 8 to 10 hours or until beef and pork are tender.

3. Remove beef and pork from cooker, using slotted spoon; place on cutting board. Shred meat with 2 forks; return to cooker. Stir in tomato paste.

4. Cover and cook on high heat setting 5 to 10 minutes or until hot.

5. Serve beef and pork mixture on buns. Meat mixture will hold on low heat setting up to 2 hours.

1 Sandwich: Calories 385 (Calories from Fat 120); Fat 13g (Saturated 5g); Cholesterol 70mg; Sodium 630mg; Carbohydrate 37g (Dietary Fiber 3g); Protein 29g • **% Daily Value:** Vitamin A 12%; Vitamin C 14%; Calcium 8%; Iron 20% • **Diet Exchanges:** 2 Starch, 3 Medium-Fat Meat, 1 Vegetable • **Carbohydrate Choices:** 2 1/2

Potluck Pointers

Whether you're feeding a hungry pack of Boy Scouts or sharing a dish with appreciative co-workers, there's no better way to satisfy a crowd than with your favorite slow cooker recipes. Everyone loves a piping-hot meal, and slow cookers make it easy to transport your food and keep it warm for serving.

Transportation Tips and Tricks

To ensure your slow cooker dish arrives in good shape:

- **Use rubber bands** or kitchen string around the handles and lid to keep the lid in place during the trip.
- **Wrap your slow cooker** in several layers of towels to keep it warm.
- **Keep the slow cooker level** when traveling to avoid spilling.
- **Plug in the slow cooker** as soon as you arrive, and set it on low to keep the food warm until serving time.

- **Mark your name** or an identifiable sign somewhere on your slow cooker. At a potluck many slow cookers look alike, so it's easy to grab the wrong one.
- **Minimize spills** during transporting by placing the slow cooker inside a large box. Stabilize the cooker with kitchen towels tucked between the cooker and box.

Go Prepared

To help out the host—and other guests—bring along:

- **Serving utensils** should be packed with your slow cooker. You will need a large serving spoon for serving mixtures, a ladle for soups or stews and tongs for ribs.
- **Serving containers** are needed for any accompaniments that go with your dish. Small bowls and spoons for toppers, basket for buns, tray or plate for breads, fruit and veggies to go with the dip and spread.

- **A small paper plate** or large napkin is nice to place next to your slow cooker on the serving table. The serving utensil can be placed on it when the lid is placed on the slow cooker to keep the food warm.
- **Take copies** of the recipe you prepared in case anyone asks you to share your culinary secrets.

Helpful Cleanup Tips

To make cleanup as effortless as possible:

- **Spray the slow cooker** with cooking spray (or lightly rub the interior with a paper towel sprinkled with vegetable oil) before cooking.
- **A removable ceramic liner** is easy to soak, and you won't have to worry about the power cord getting wet. It can even go into the dishwasher.

- **Completely cool** the slow cooker before adding water for cleanup to prevent cracking the ceramic interior.
- **Timing is key.** The sooner you start cleanup, the less chance food has of sticking permanently to your appliance.

Tasty Take-Alongs

Not sure what to bring to your next potluck party? Here are some surefire winners for any occasion that are especially good to tote to these suggested events.

Event	Appetizers, Snacks or Sides	Beef	Chicken	Ham/Pork
Baby Shower	Party Crab Dip (page 16)	Asian Meatballs (page 178)	Chicken-Wild Rice Casserole with Dried Cherries (page 69)	Ham and Lentil Stew (page 90)
Book Club	Hot Artichoke and Spinach Dip (page 14)	Beef au Jus Sandwiches (page 166)	Teriyaki Barbecued Chicken Sandwiches (page 160)	Pork Tortilla Soup (page 47)
Boy/Girl Scouts Meeting	Hot Dog and Bacon Roll-Ups (page 25)	Pizza Joe Sandwiches (page 170)	White Chili with Chicken (page 61)	Barbecued Beef and Pork Sandwiches (page 163)
Bridal Shower	Cheesy Chicken and Peppers Dip (page 18)	Zesty Italian Beef Tips (page 80)	Spicy Chicken in Peanut Sauce (page 100)	Honey-Dijon Ham (page 126)
Children's Birthday Party	Sausage and Pepperoni Dip (page 22)	Slow-Simmered Spaghetti Meat Sauce (page 113)	Chicken and Vegetable Tortellini Stew (page 50)	Ham with Cheesy Potatoes (page 88)
Cocktail Party	Sherry Buttered Mushrooms (page 145)	French Onion Meatballs (page 28)	Asian Chicken Drummies (page 23)	Teriyaki Smoked Riblets (page 32)
Family Reunion	Easy Savory Baked Beans (page 136)	Swedish Meatballs (page 180)	Chicken and Bean Tacos (page 162)	Smoky Ham and Navy Bean Stew (page 49)
Football Playoffs	Chex® Party Mix (page 34)	Crowd-Pleasing Chili (page 172)	Chicken Stew (page 68)	Hot and Spicy Riblets (page 31)
Holiday Party	Honey-Cranberry Butternut Squash (page 210)	Provençal Beef with Zinfandel (page 196)	Holiday Chicken Alfredo (page 188)	Spiced Orange Pork Roast (page 200)
School Event	Spanish Rice with Tomatoes and Peppers (page 142)	Beef and Creamy Potato Casserole (page 116)	Creamy Chicken and Wild Rice Soup (page 39)	Curried Pork Stew (page 58)
Wedding Anniversary	Smoky Bacon and Gruyère Dip (page 13)	Rosemary-Garlic Beef Roast (page 198)	Chicken Breasts with Mushroom Cream Sauce (page 190)	Barbecued Pork Chops (page 122)
Work Party	Hot Nacho Bean Dip (page 12)	Mexican Beef Chili (page 63)	Sweet-and-Sour Chicken (page 94)	Southwestern Pork Burritos (page 168)

Beef au Jus Sandwiches

12 sandwiches

SLOW COOKER:
3 1/2- to 4-quart

PREP TIME:
15 minutes

COOK TIME:
Low 8 to 10 hours

HOLD TIME:
Low up to 4 hours

Betty's Success Tip

Au jus is a French term for serving meat with its own natural juices. We've added the balsamic vinegar to tenderize the meat and add even more flavor.

Serving Suggestions

Cans of root beer, store-bought potato salad and already-sliced fresh fruit from the grocery store will complete this meal, perfect for a picnic in the park.

1 large sweet onion (Bermuda, Maui, Spanish, Walla Walla), sliced

1 can (14 ounces) beef broth

4-pound beef boneless rump roast, trimmed of fat

2 tablespoons balsamic vinegar

1 envelope (0.7 ounce) Italian dressing mix

1/2 teaspoon salt

1/4 teaspoon black pepper

12 hoagie buns, split

1 large green bell pepper, thinly sliced

12 slices (1 ounce each) provolone cheese, cut in half

1. Place onion slices and broth in 3 1/2- to 4-quart slow cooker. Brush all surfaces of beef roast with vinegar. Place on onions. Sprinkle with dressing mix (dry), salt and pepper.

2. Cover and cook on low heat setting 8 to 10 hours or until beef is tender.

3. About 5 minutes before serving, remove beef from cooker; place on cutting board. Cut beef across grain into thin slices; return slices to cooker and mix well.

4. Serve beef mixture on buns with bell pepper and cheese. Beef mixture will hold on low heat setting up to 4 hours.

1 Sandwich: Calories 525 (Calories from Fat 135); Fat 15g (Saturated 7g); Cholesterol 105mg; Sodium 1370mg; Carbohydrate 52g (Dietary Fiber 3g); Protein 46g • **% Daily Value:** Vitamin A 8%; Vitamin C 10%; Calcium 28%; Iron 30% • **Diet Exchanges:** 3 1/2 Starch, 5 Lean Meat • **Carbohydrate Choices:** 3 1/2

Beef au Jus Sandwiches

Southwestern Pork Burritos

12 burritos

SLOW COOKER:
3 1/2- to 4-quart

PREP TIME:
15 minutes

COOK TIME:
Low 8 to 10 hours

HOLD TIME:
Low up to 2 hours

Betty's Success Tip

To warm tortillas, wrap them in aluminum foil and heat in a 325° oven for about 15 minutes. Or place on a microwavable paper towel, and microwave on High for 30 seconds.

Serving Suggestion

This tasty pork filling also makes great sandwiches. Spoon the filling on top of toasted bread slices. Top with shredded lettuce and shredded Monterey Jack or Cheddar cheese.

2 1/2-pound well-trimmed pork boneless shoulder roast

1 can (10 ounces) diced tomatoes and green chilies, undrained

3 tablespoons tomato paste

1 tablespoon honey

3 cloves garlic, finely chopped

1 tablespoon chili powder

1/4 teaspoon salt

12 flour tortillas (8 to 10 inches in diameter)

Assorted toppings (such as shredded Cheddar cheese, sour cream, chopped fresh cilantro, shredded lettuce, diced tomatoes), if desired

1. Place pork in 3 1/2- to 4-quart slow cooker.

2. Place tomatoes, tomato paste, honey, garlic, chili powder and salt in blender. Cover and blend on medium-high speed 10 seconds, stopping blender frequently to scrape sides. Pour over pork.

3. Cover and cook on low heat setting 8 to 10 hours or until pork is very tender.

4. Remove pork from cooker; place on cutting board. Shred pork with 2 forks; return to cooker and mix well.

5. Serve pork mixture with tortillas and toppings. Pork mixture will hold on low heat setting up to 2 hours.

1 Burrito: Calories 330 (Calories from Fat 135); Fat 15g (Saturated 5g); Cholesterol 60mg; Sodium 390mg; Carbohydrate 28g (Dietary Fiber 2g); Protein 24g • **% Daily Value:** Vitamin A 6%; Vitamin C 4%; Calcium 6%; Iron 12% • **Diet Exchanges:** 2 Starch, 2 1/2 Medium-Fat Meat • **Carbohydrate Choices:** 2

Southwestern Pork Burritos

Pizza Joe Sandwiches

18 servings

SLOW COOKER:
3 1/2- to 4-quart

PREP TIME:
15 minutes

COOK TIME:
Low 4 to 6 hours

HOLD TIME:
Low up to 4 hours

Ingredient Substitution

Just as for pizza, the meat in these sandwiches can be interchanged according to your family's personal preferences. Use all bulk Italian sausage (be sure to cook until no longer pink), or use half ground beef and half Italian sausage.

Serving Suggestion

To make this kid-friendly recipe all the more appealing, serve with a take-along treat such as pudding snacks or chewy fruit snack rolls.

2 pounds lean ground beef

1 large onion, chopped (1 cup)

1 small green bell pepper, chopped (1/2 cup)

2 jars (14 ounces each) pizza sauce

1 package (3 1/2 ounces) sliced pepperoni, chopped (3/4 cup)

1 teaspoon dried basil leaves

1/2 teaspoon dried oregano leaves

18 sandwich buns, split

2 cups shredded mozzarella cheese (8 ounces)

1. Cook beef and onion in 12-inch skillet over medium-high heat about 8 minutes, stirring frequently, until beef is brown; drain.

2. Spray 3 1/2- to 4-quart slow cooker with cooking spray. Spoon beef mixture into cooker. Stir in bell pepper, pizza sauce, pepperoni, basil and oregano.

3. Cover and cook on low heat setting 4 to 6 hours.

4. Serve beef mixture with buns and cheese. Beef mixture will hold on low heat setting up to 4 hours.

1 Sandwich: Calories 320 (Calories from Fat 145); Fat 16g (Saturated 6g); Cholesterol 40mg; Sodium 650mg; Carbohydrate 27g (Dietary Fiber 2g); Protein 18g • **% Daily Value:** Vitamin A 6%; Vitamin C 12%; Calcium 16%; Iron 14% • **Diet Exchanges:** 2 Starch, 1 1/2 Medium-Fat Meat, 1 1/2 Fat • **Carbohydrate Choices:** 2

Turkey Chili

10 servings (1 1/3 cups each)

Photo on page 158

SLOW COOKER:
5- to 6-quart

PREP TIME:
20 minutes

COOK TIME:
Low 7 to 8 hours

HOLD TIME:
Low up to 4 hours

Betty's Success Tip

There's a surprise ingredient in this recipe—cornmeal. It's a delicious addition that thickens the chili with Tex-Mex pizzazz.

Ingredient Substitution

Mix and match the flavors of this chili by using black beans instead of pinto beans or ground beef instead of the ground turkey.

2 1/2 pounds ground turkey

2 large onions, chopped (2 cups)

1 large green bell pepper, chopped (1 1/2 cups)

1 can (28 ounces) diced tomatoes, undrained

2 cans (15 1/2 ounces each) pinto beans, undrained

1 can (14 ounces) seasoned chicken broth with roasted garlic

2 cans (4 1/2 ounces each) diced green chiles, undrained

1/3 cup cornmeal

1 tablespoon chili powder

1 tablespoon dried oregano leaves

2 teaspoons ground cumin

1 teaspoon salt

1. Cook turkey in 12-inch skillet over medium-high heat 5 to 8 minutes, stirring frequently, until no longer pink; drain.

2. Mix turkey, onions, bell pepper, tomatoes, pinto beans, broth and chiles in 5- to 6-quart slow cooker. Mix remaining ingredients in small bowl; stir into turkey mixture.

3. Cover and cook on low heat setting 7 to 8 hours or until chili is thickened and bubbling. Chili will hold on low heat setting up to 4 hours. If chili becomes too thick while holding, stir in up to 1/2 cup hot water to thin.

1 Serving: Calories 345 (Calories from Fat 70); Fat 8g (Saturated 2g); Cholesterol 5mg; Sodium 660mg; Carbohydrate 35g (Dietary Fiber 10g); Protein 35g • **% Daily Value:** Vitamin A 16%; Vitamin C 32%; Calcium 10%; Iron 26% • **Diet Exchanges:** 2 Starch, 4 Very Lean Meat, 1 Vegetable, 1/2 Fat • **Carbohydrate Choices:** 2

Crowd-Pleasing Chili

12 servings (1 1/3 cups each)

SLOW COOKER:
5- to 6-quart

PREP TIME:
20 minutes

COOK TIME:
Low 8 to 10 hours

HOLD TIME:
Low up to 2 hours

Betty's Success Tip

Always brown ground beef just before adding it to the slow cooker. Starting with hot meat helps the mixture reach a safe internal temperature more quickly. By browning the beef first, you also eliminate the extra fat and liquid that would accumulate during cooking.

Ingredient Substitution

If you like your chili hot and spicy, use a pound of ground beef and a pound of hot and spicy bulk pork or Italian beef sausage instead of all beef. Cook and drain the two together before adding to the cooker.

2 pounds lean ground beef

2 large onions, chopped (2 cups)

1 can (28 ounces) diced tomatoes, undrained

2 cans (15 ounces each) seasoned tomato sauce for chili

2 cans (15 1/2 ounces each) kidney beans, undrained

2 cans (15 ounces each) spicy chili beans

1 tablespoon honey

1 1/2 teaspoons ground cumin

1 teaspoon chili powder

1. Cook beef and onions in 12-inch skillet or 4-quart Dutch oven over medium-high heat about 10 minutes, stirring occasionally, until beef is brown; drain.

2. Mix beef mixture and remaining ingredients in 5- to 6-quart slow cooker.

3. Cover and cook on low heat setting 8 to 10 hours or until chili is hot and bubbly. Chili will hold on low heat setting up to 2 hours.

1 Serving: Calories 330 (Calories from Fat 110); Fat 12g (Saturated 4g); Cholesterol 45mg; Sodium 1015mg; Carbohydrate 39g (Dietary Fiber 9g); Protein 25g • **% Daily Value:** Vitamin A 14%; Vitamin C 22%; Calcium 8%; Iron 30% • **Diet Exchanges:** 2 Starch, 2 Lean Meat, 2 Vegetable • **Carbohydrate Choices:** 2 1/2

Hamburger Hash

12 servings (1 cup each)

SLOW COOKER:
5- to 6-quart

PREP TIME:
20 minutes

COOK TIME:
Low 8 to 9 hours

HOLD TIME:
Low up to 2 hours

Betty's Success Tip

O'Brien potatoes are made of diced potatoes, chopped onions and pimientos. Some-times red or green bell pep-pers are used in place of the pimientos. For tender potatoes, make sure to thaw them before adding to the slow cooker.

Serving Suggestions

This recipe is a tried-and-true kid pleaser. Take it to Cub Scouts, Girl Scouts or school events, and there's little chance you'll have leftovers.

3 pounds lean ground beef

1 can (15 ounces) tomato puree

1 can (10 3/4 ounces) condensed cream of mushroom soup

1 can (10 1/2 ounces) condensed French onion soup with beef stock

3/4 cup water

1 bag (28 ounces) frozen O'Brien potatoes with onions and peppers, thawed

4 medium carrots, diced (2 cups)

1 teaspoon salt

1. Cook beef in 12-inch skillet over medium-high heat about 10 minutes, stirring occasionally, until brown; drain.

2. Mix tomato puree and mushroom soup in medium bowl. Stir in onion soup and water.

3. Spray 5- to 6-quart slow cooker with cooking spray. Reserve 1 cup of the potatoes. Gently mix beef, remaining potatoes, carrots, salt and soup mixture in cooker. Sprinkle with reserved 1 cup potatoes.

4. Cover and cook on low heat setting 8 to 9 hours or until vegetables are tender. Hash will hold on low heat setting up to 2 hours.

1 Serving: Calories 395 (Calories from Fat 215); Fat 24g (Saturated 8g); Cholesterol 65mg; Sodium 950mg; Carbohydrate 24g (Dietary Fiber 5g); Protein 26g • **% Daily Value:** Vitamin A 82%; Vitamin C 14%; Calcium 4%; Iron 16% • **Diet Exchanges:** 1 1/2 Starch, 3 Medium-Fat Meat, 1 Fat • **Carbohydrate Choices:** 1 1/2

Chicken and Sausage Jambalaya

10 servings (1 1/2 cups each)

SLOW COOKER:
5- to 6-quart

PREP TIME:
15 minutes

COOK TIME:
Low 8 to 10 hours

FINISHING COOK TIME:
Low 15 minutes

HOLD TIME:
Low up to 1 hour

Ingredient Substitution

Andouille sausage, a spicy smoked sausage, is often used in Cajun cooking. It may be used as a substitute for the Polish sausage in this recipe.

Serving Suggestion

If you prefer more "heat," sprinkle red pepper sauce on this Cajun favorite just before serving. You can also top with fresh parsley for added color.

2 large onions, chopped (2 cups)

1 large green bell pepper, chopped (1 1/2 cups)

2 medium stalks celery, chopped (1 cup)

2 1/2 pounds boneless, skinless chicken thighs

1 tablespoon Cajun seasoning

1 pound fully cooked Polish sausage links, cut into 1 1/2-inch pieces

1 can (28 ounces) diced tomatoes, undrained

1 can (14 ounces) chicken broth

1 package (14 ounces) instant long-grain rice

1. Place onions, bell pepper and celery in 5- to 6-quart slow cooker. Top with chicken; sprinkle with Cajun seasoning. Top with sausage, tomatoes and broth.

2. Cover and cook on low heat setting 8 to 10 hours or until juice of chicken is no longer pink when centers of thickest pieces are cut.

3. Gently stir uncooked rice into chicken mixture. Cover and cook on low heat setting about 15 minutes or until rice is tender. Jambalaya will hold on low heat setting up to 1 hour.

1 Serving: Calories 525 (Calories from Fat 200); Fat 22g (Saturated 8g); Cholesterol 95mg; Sodium 830mg; Carbohydrate 47g (Dietary Fiber 2g); Protein 35g • **% Daily Value:** Vitamin A 8%; Vitamin C 22%; Calcium 8%; Iron 26% • **Diet Exchanges:** 3 Starch, 3 1/2 Medium-Fat Meat, 1/2 Fat • **Carbohydrate Choices:** 3

Crock-Pot®
Stoneware Slow Cooker

Off   Low   High

Chicken and Sausage Jambalaya

Make-Your-Own Taco Salad

12 servings

SLOW COOKER:
3 1/2- to 4-quart

PREP TIME:
25 minutes

COOK TIME:
Low 6 to 8 hours

HOLD TIME:
Low up to 4 hours

Betty's Success Tip

In the (unlikely!) event there is any beef mixture left, bring it home and refrigerate it for lunch the next day. Reheat the beef mixture, wrap in a flour tortilla and serve with fresh toppings.

Ingredient Substitution

If ripe avocados aren't available, take along two containers of purchased guacamole instead.

2 pounds lean ground beef

1 large onion, chopped (1 cup)

2 envelopes (1 1/4 ounces each) taco seasoning mix

2 cans (15 1/2 ounces each) pinto beans, drained

2 cans (15 ounces each) tomato sauce

1/4 teaspoon pepper, if desired

12 cups shredded lettuce

4 cups corn chips

4 medium tomatoes, chopped (3 cups)

2 medium avocados, pitted, peeled and chopped

3 cups shredded American or Cheddar cheese (12 ounces)

1 1/2 cups salsa

1. Cook beef and onion in 12-inch skillet over medium-high heat about 8 minutes, stirring frequently, until beef is brown; drain.

2. Spray 3 1/2- to 4-quart slow cooker with cooking spray. Mix beef mixture, taco seasoning mix, beans, tomato sauce and pepper in cooker.

3. Cover and cook on low heat setting 6 to 8 hours.

4. To serve, place lettuce and corn chips on individual plates. Top each with beef mixture, tomatoes, avocados, cheese and salsa. Beef mixture will hold on low heat setting up to 4 hours.

1 Serving: Calories 505 (Calories from Fat 250); Fat 28g (Saturated 11g); Cholesterol 70mg; Sodium 1240mg; Carbohydrate 42g (Dietary Fiber 12g); Protein 31g • **% Daily Value:** Vitamin A 44%; Vitamin C 52%; Calcium 24%; Iron 30% • **Diet Exchanges:** 2 Starch, 3 Medium-Fat Meat, 2 Vegetable, 2 Fat • **Carbohydrate Choices:** 3

Beef and Green Chile Tortilla Dinner

12 servings

SLOW COOKER:
3 1/2- to 4-quart

PREP TIME:
20 minutes

COOK TIME:
Low 8 to 10 hours

HOLD TIME:
Low up to 2 hours

Betty's Success Tip

Capsaicin, which is concentrated mainly in the seeds and veins, causes the "heat" in chiles. Removing the seeds of the chiles helps reduce the spiciness of this slow-cooked casserole.

Serving Suggestion

Let everyone "personalize" their serving of this delightful Mexican dish by providing small bowls filled with toppings such as tomatoes, sour cream, Cheddar cheese and ripe olives.

2 pounds lean ground beef

2 large onions, chopped (2 cups)

1 envelope (1 1/4 ounces) reduced-sodium taco seasoning mix

1/4 cup water

4 cans (4 ounces each) peeled whole mild green chiles

1 can (16 ounces) refried beans

1 jar (16 ounces) mild thick-and-chunky salsa

12 cups bite-size tortilla chips

2 bags (8 ounces each) shredded Mexican 4-cheese blend (4 cups)

1. Cook beef and onion in 12-inch skillet over medium-high heat about 10 minutes, stirring occasionally, until beef is brown; drain. Return beef mixture to skillet; stir in taco seasoning mix and water.

2. Spray 3 1/2- to 4-quart slow cooker with cooking spray. Cut chiles in half; remove seeds. Arrange half of the chiles evenly over bottom of cooker. Spoon in beef mixture. Spoon refried beans over beef in an even layer. Top with remaining chiles. Pour salsa over all.

3. Cover and cook on low heat setting 8 to 10 hours or until bubbling. For each serving, place about 1 cup tortilla chips on plate, spoon ground beef mixture over chips and top with about 1/3 cup of the cheese. Ground beef mixture will hold on low heat setting up to 2 hours. Stir occasionally.

1 Serving: Calories 540 (Calories from Fat 295); Fat 33g (Saturated 13g); Cholesterol 95mg; Sodium 970mg; Carbohydrate 31g (Dietary Fiber 6g); Protein 36g • **% Daily Value:** Vitamin A 24%; Vitamin C 18%; Calcium 30%; Iron 24% • **Diet Exchanges:** 2 Starch, 4 Medium-Fat Meat, 2 Fat • **Carbohydrate Choices:** 2

Asian Meatballs

12 servings (3 meatballs each)

SLOW COOKER:
3 1/2- to 4-quart

PREP TIME:
20 minutes

BAKE TIME:
30 minutes

COOK TIME:
Low 2 to 4 hours

HOLD TIME:
Low up to 2 hours

Betty's Success Tip

Water chestnuts, a popular ingredient in Asian cooking, add a little crunch to these meatballs. You can find canned water chestnuts in the ethnic foods aisle of most supermarkets.

Serving Suggestion

These flavorful meatballs are also great to serve as appetizers. Fill a tall glass with bamboo skewers or a short one with toothpicks and let your guests help themselves.

1 pound lean ground beef

1/2 cup finely chopped water chestnuts

1/3 cup plain bread crumbs

1/4 cup milk

1 tablespoon soy sauce

1/2 teaspoon garlic salt

4 medium green onions, sliced (1/4 cup)

1 egg, slightly beaten

1/2 cup barbecue sauce

1/4 cup plum sauce

2 tablespoons hoisin sauce

1. Heat oven to 375°. Spray jelly roll pan, 15 1/2 × 10 1/2 × 1 inch, with cooking spray. Mix beef, water chestnuts, bread crumbs, milk, soy sauce, salt, green onions and egg in large bowl. Shape into about 36 meatballs, 1 inch in diameter. Place in pan.

2. Bake uncovered 25 to 30 minutes or until meatballs are no longer pink in center and juice of beef is clear.

3. Spray 3 1/2- to 4-quart slow cooker with cooking spray. Place meatballs in cooker. Mix together remaining ingredients and gently stir into meatballs.

4. Cover and cook on low heat setting 2 to 4 hours or until hot. Meatballs will hold on low heat setting up to 2 hours.

1 Serving: Calories 125 (Calories from Fat 55); Fat 6g (Saturated 2g); Cholesterol 40mg; Sodium 330mg; Carbohydrate 9g (Dietary Fiber 0g); Protein 9g • **% Daily Value:** Vitamin A 2%; Vitamin C 2%; Calcium 2%; Iron 6% • **Diet Exchanges:** 1/2 Starch, 1 Medium-Fat Meat, 1/2 Fat • **Carbohydrate Choices:** 1/2

Asian Meatballs

Swedish Meatballs

12 servings (5 meatballs each)

SLOW COOKER:
5- to 6-quart

PREP TIME:
1 hour 5 minutes

COOK TIME:
Low 3 to 4 hours

HOLD TIME:
Low up to 2 hours

Ingredient Substitution

Used up the last of your dry bread crumbs? Finely crushed cracker crumbs or corn flakes, or quick-cooking or old-fashioned oats will work in place of dry bread crumbs.

Serving Suggestion

Leftover meatballs? Make a box of flavored mashed potatoes, heat the meatballs in their sauce and spoon over the potatoes. Serve this quick and easy meal with buttered sliced beets.

1 1/2 cups milk

4 eggs

1 1/2 cups plain dry bread crumbs

1/4 cup instant minced onion

2 teaspoons ground mustard

2 teaspoons celery salt

1 teaspoon ground nutmeg

1 teaspoon salt

1 teaspoon pepper

4 pounds lean ground beef

3 cans (10 3/4 ounces each) condensed cream of mushroom soup

1 1/2 cups water

1 teaspoon dried dill weed, if desired

1. Heat oven to 375°. Spray 2 rectangular pans, 15 1/2 × 10 1/2 × 1 inch, with cooking spray.

2. Beat milk and eggs in large bowl with wire whisk until blended. Stir in bread crumbs, onion, mustard, celery salt, nutmeg, salt and pepper. Mix in beef until well blended. Shape mixture into 60 meatballs, about 2 inches in diameter; place in pans. Bake uncovered about 30 minutes or until no longer pink in center and juice is clear.

3. Spray 5- to 6-quart slow cooker with cooking spray. Transfer meatballs to cooker. Mix soup, water and dill weed in large bowl; pour over meatballs. Stir to coat meatballs with sauce.

4. Cover and cook on low heat setting 3 to 4 hours or until meatballs are very tender and sauce is bubbling. Meatballs will hold on low heat setting up to 2 hours. If sauce becomes too thick while holding, stir in up to 1/2 cup hot water. Stir well before serving.

1 Serving: Calories 465 (Calories from Fat 260); Fat 29g (Saturated 11g); Cholesterol 160mg; Sodium 1200mg; Carbohydrate 17g (Dietary Fiber 1g); Protein 34g • **% Daily Value:** Vitamin A 6%; Vitamin C 0%; Calcium 12%; Iron 22% • **Diet Exchanges:** 1 Starch, 4 1/2 Medium-Fat Meat, 1 Fat • **Carbohydrate Choices:** 1

Texas-Style Barbecued Beans

12 servings (1/2 cup each)

SLOW COOKER:
3 1/2- to 4-quart

PREP TIME:
15 minutes

COOK TIME:
Low 4 to 6 hours

HOLD TIME:
Low up to 2 hours

Betty's Success Tip

Bacon is a snap to prepare in the microwave. Simply place the bacon slices between two microwavable paper towels on a microwavable plate, and microwave on High 30 to 60 seconds for each slice.

Serving Suggestion

When transporting beans to a potluck, wrap the slow cooker in several layers of towels to keep it warm. Use rubber bands or kitchen string around the handles and lid to keep the lid in place during the trip. When you arrive, plug in the cooker and set it on low to keep the beans warm.

3 slices bacon

2 cans (15 1/2 ounces each) great northern beans, drained and rinsed

2 cans (15 ounces each) black beans, drained and rinsed

2 cloves garlic, finely chopped

1 medium onion, chopped (1/2 cup)

3/4 cup ketchup

1/4 cup packed brown sugar

1/4 cup barbecue sauce

1 tablespoon yellow mustard

1 tablespoon Worcestershire sauce

2 teaspoons chili powder

1/4 teaspoon red pepper sauce

1. Cook bacon in 8-inch skillet over medium heat, turning occasionally, until crisp. Remove bacon from skillet; drain on paper towels.

2. Gently mix remaining ingredients in 3 1/2- to 4-quart slow cooker. Crumble bacon; sprinkle over bean mixture.

3. Cover and cook on low heat setting 4 to 6 hours. Beans will hold on low heat setting up to 2 hours.

1 Serving: Calories 270 (Calories from Fat 20); Fat 2g (Saturated 0g); Cholesterol 0mg; Sodium 570mg; Carbohydrate 49g (Dietary Fiber 10g); Protein 14g • **% Daily Value:** Vitamin A 6%; Vitamin C 2%; Calcium 12%; Iron 26% • **Diet Exchanges:** 3 Starch, 1/2 Very Lean Meat, 1/2 Fat • **Carbohydrate Choices:** 3

Southwestern Calico Baked Beans

20 servings (1/2 cup each)

SLOW COOKER:
3 1/2- to 4-quart

PREP TIME:
15 minutes

COOK TIME:
Low 4 to 6 hours

HOLD TIME:
Low up to 2 hours

1 package (12 ounces) bulk hot pork sausage

1 can (15 ounces) baked beans, drained

1 package (9 ounces) frozen baby lima beans

1 can (15 ounces) black-eyed peas, drained

1 can (15 1/2 ounces) dark red kidney beans, drained

1 cup salsa

1 envelope (1 1/4 ounces) taco seasoning mix

Betty's Success Tip

This southwestern version of pork and baked beans is a great dish to bring to a potluck. The hot pork sausage, salsa and taco seasoning add a special zing to this popular bean dish.

Serving Suggestion

Ask someone else invited to the potluck to make rice, and place the beans and rice next to each other at the table.

1. Cook sausage in 10-inch skillet over medium heat, stirring occasionally, about 8 minutes or until no longer pink; drain.

2. Spray 3 1/2- to 4-quart slow cooker with cooking spray. Add sausage to cooker. Gently stir in remaining ingredients.

3. Cover and cook on low heat setting 4 to 6 hours or until hot and bubbly. Beans will hold on low heat setting up to 2 hours.

1 Serving: Calories 150 (Calories from Fat 35); Fat 4g (Saturated 1g); Cholesterol 12mg; Sodium 680mg; Carbohydrate 29g (Dietary Fiber 7g); Protein 10g • **% Daily Value:** Vitamin A 20%; Vitamin C 6%; Calcium 6%; Iron 22% • **Diet Exchanges:** 2 Starch • **Carbohydrate Choices:** 2

Baked Potato Bar

12 servings

SLOW COOKER:
5- to 6-quart

PREP TIME:
10 minutes

COOK TIME:
Low 6 to 8 hours

HOLD TIME:
Low up to 2 hours

Betty's Success Tip

Brushing the potatoes with oil before cooking is a good way to make the salt and pepper cling, for those who like to eat their potato skin.

Serving Suggestion

Here's an easy after-work party for a Friday night! Cook the potatoes all day in the slow cooker. When you get home, set out some additional hearty toppings, like chopped ham, small cooked shrimp or chili, and let everyone help themselves!

12 unpeeled russet potatoes (6 to 8 ounces each)

2 tablespoons olive or vegetable oil

1 1/2 teaspoons salt

1 teaspoon coarse black pepper

Assorted toppings (such as sour cream, ranch dip, chopped bell pepper, bacon bits, assorted shredded cheeses, crumbled blue cheese, chopped green onions, salsa), if desired

1. Pierce potatoes with fork. Place potatoes and oil in large plastic food-storage bag; toss to coat with oil. Sprinkle with salt and pepper. Wrap potatoes individually in aluminum foil; place in 5- to 6-quart slow cooker.

2. Cover and cook on low heat setting 6 to 8 hours or until potatoes are tender.

3. Serve potatoes with toppings. Potatoes will hold on low heat setting up to 2 hours.

1 Serving: Calories 155 (Calories from Fat 20); Fat 2g (Saturated 0g); Cholesterol 0mg; Sodium 310mg; Carbohydrate 31g (Dietary Fiber 3g); Protein 3g • **% Daily Value:** Vitamin A 0%; Vitamin C 12%; Calcium 0%; Iron 8% • **Diet Exchanges:** 1 Starch, 1 Fruit • **Carbohydrate Choices:** 2

Cheesy Ravioli Casserole

10 servings

SLOW COOKER:
5- to 6-quart

PREP TIME:
15 minutes

COOK TIME:
Low 5 1/2 to 6 1/2 hours

HOLD TIME:
Low up to 30 minutes

Ingredient Substitution

Turn this cheesy pasta dish into a great vegetarian meal by using cheese-filled ravioli instead of the beef-filled ravioli.

Serving Suggestion

Take a loaf of crusty garlic bread to serve with this family-pleasing pasta dish. A bag of mixed salad greens and a bottle of salad dressing makes this a very quick and easy meal to take with you.

1 tablespoon olive or vegetable oil

1 medium onion, chopped (1/2 cup)

1 large clove garlic, finely chopped

2 jars (26 ounces each) four cheese–flavored tomato pasta sauce

1 can (15 ounces) tomato sauce

1 teaspoon dried Italian seasoning

2 packages (25 ounces each) frozen beef-filled ravioli

2 cups shredded mozzarella cheese (8 ounces)

1/4 cup chopped fresh parsley, if desired

1. Heat oil in 4-quart Dutch oven or 12-inch skillet over medium heat. Cook onion and garlic in oil about 4 minutes, stirring occasionally, until onion is tender. Stir in pasta sauce, tomato sauce and Italian seasoning.

2. Spray 5- to 6-quart slow cooker with cooking spray. Place 1 cup of the sauce mixture in cooker. Add 1 package frozen ravioli; top with 1 cup of the cheese. Top with remaining package of ravioli and 1 cup cheese. Pour remaining sauce mixture over top.

3. Cover and cook on low heat setting 5 hours 30 minutes to 6 hours 30 minutes. Sprinkle with parsley before serving. Ravioli will hold on low heat setting up to 30 minutes.

1 Serving: Calories 500 (Calories from Fat 160); Fat 18g (Saturated 8g); Cholesterol 175mg; Sodium 2110mg; Carbohydrate 57g (Dietary Fiber 5g); Protein 26g • **% Daily Value:** Vitamin A 74%; Vitamin C 26%; Calcium 38%; Iron 24% • **Diet Exchanges:** 4 Starch, 2 Medium-Fat Meat, 2 Fat • **Carbohydrate Choices:** 4

BettyCrocker.com

Cheesy Ravioli Casserole

Hassle-Free
Holidays

7

- Holiday Chicken Alfredo 188
- Chicken Breasts with Mushroom Cream Sauce 190
- Maple- and Apricot-Sauced Turkey Breast 191
- Bacon- and Corn Bread–Stuffed Turkey Breast 194
- Provençal Beef with Zinfandel 196
- Rosemary-Garlic Beef Roast 198
- Spinach- and Mushroom-Stuffed Pork Roast 199
- Spiced Orange Pork Roast 200
- Ham with Currant-Cherry Sauce 201
- Apple-Walnut Stuffing 202
- Pear-Apple Sauce with Cherries 203
- Garlic-Parmesan Smashed Potatoes 204
- Creamed Potatoes with Garden Peas 206
- Smoky Cheese and Potato Bake 207
- Sweet Potatoes with Orange-Pecan Butter 208
- Honey-Cranberry Butternut Squash 210
- Southwest Vegetable Stew 211

◀ **Ham with Currant-Cherry Sauce (page 201)**

Holiday Chicken Alfredo

5 servings

SLOW COOKER:
3 1/2- to 4-quart

PREP TIME:
15 minutes

COOK TIME:
Low 5 to 6 hours

FINISHING COOK TIME:
High 20 minutes

Betty's Success Tip

Alfredo sauce is available in jars in the pasta sauce section. You can also find Alfredo sauce in the refrigerator or dairy case, next to the fresh pasta; you'll need to use one and a half 10-ounce containers instead.

Serving Suggestion

When you invite friends over for dinner, you can serve this creamy chicken with a warm baguette and a spinach salad tossed with strawberries and a red-wine vinaigrette.

1 1/4 pounds boneless, skinless chicken thighs (about 6 thighs), cut into 3/4-inch pieces

1 jar (4 1/2 ounces) sliced mushrooms, drained

1/2 cup drained roasted red bell pepper strips (from 7-ounce jar)

2 tablespoons dry sherry, if desired

1 jar (16 ounces) Alfredo pasta sauce

3 cups frozen broccoli cuts

10 ounces uncooked fettuccine

2 tablespoons shredded fresh Parmesan cheese

1. Layer chicken, mushrooms and bell pepper strips in 3 1/2- to 4-quart slow cooker. Drizzle with sherry. Pour pasta sauce evenly over top.

2. Cover and cook on low heat setting 5 to 6 hours.

3. About 25 minutes before serving, rinse broccoli with warm water to thaw; drain well. Stir broccoli into chicken mixture. Cover and cook on high heat setting 20 minutes. Meanwhile, cook and drain fettuccine as directed on package.

4. Just before serving, stir cooked fettuccine into chicken mixture. Sprinkle with cheese.

1 Serving: Calories 750 (Calories from Fat 385); Fat 43g (Saturated 23g); Cholesterol 215mg; Sodium 660mg; Carbohydrate 52g (Dietary Fiber 6g); Protein 44g • **% Daily Value:** Vitamin A 82%; Vitamin C 62%; Calcium 38%; Iron 30% • **Diet Exchanges:** 3 Starch, 4 1/2 Lean Meat, 1 Vegetable, 6 Fat • **Carbohydrate Choices:** 3 1/2

Holiday Chicken Alfredo

Chicken Breasts with Mushroom Cream Sauce

12 servings

SLOW COOKER:
5- to 6-quart

PREP TIME:
20 minutes

COOK TIME:
Low 4 to 5 hours

FINISHING COOK TIME:
High 10 to 15 minutes

Betty's Success Tip

Chicken breasts are not often recommended for use in slow cooker recipes because they tend to dry out and become stringy. That's not the case with this recipe. The chicken breasts stay moist because they are smothered with creamy sauce and cook just 4 to 5 hours.

Ingredient Substitution

If baby portabella mushrooms aren't readily available, sliced button mushrooms will also work in this delicious dish.

1 tablespoon butter or margarine

1 medium leek, sliced (1 cup)

2 cups sliced baby portabella mushrooms

12 boneless, skinless chicken breast halves (about 3 3/4 pounds)

1 teaspoon seasoned salt

1/2 teaspoon coarsely ground pepper

1/4 cup chicken broth

1/4 cup dry white wine

1 tablespoon Dijon mustard

1/2 cup half-and-half

1/4 cup all-purpose flour

1/4 cup sliced drained roasted red bell peppers (from 7-ounce jar)

1. Melt butter in 12-inch nonstick skillet over medium heat. Cook leek in butter 2 minutes, stirring occasionally. Stir in mushrooms. Cook 2 minutes, stirring occasionally. Remove mushroom mixture from skillet.

2. Sprinkle both sides of chicken with seasoned salt and pepper. Cook chicken in skillet 3 to 5 minutes or until browned on both sides. Layer chicken and mushroom mixture in 5- to 6-quart slow cooker. Mix broth, wine and mustard; pour over chicken and mushrooms.

3. Cover and cook on low heat setting 4 to 5 hours or until juice of chicken is no longer pink when centers of thickest pieces are cut.

4. Remove chicken from cooker; cover to keep warm. Mix half-and-half and flour until smooth; stir into mixture in cooker. Cover and cook on high heat setting 10 to 15 minutes, stirring occasionally, until mixture thickens. Stir in bell peppers. Serve sauce with chicken.

1 Serving: Calories 185 (Calories from Fat 55); Fat 6g (Saturated 2g); Cholesterol 80mg; Sodium 250mg; Carbohydrate 4g (Dietary Fiber 0g); Protein 28g • **% Daily Value:** Vitamin A 6%; Vitamin C 6%; Calcium 2%; Iron 6% • **Diet Exchanges:** 4 Very Lean Meat, 1 Fat • **Carbohydrate Choices:** 0

Maple- and Apricot-Sauced Turkey Breast

8 to 10 servings

SLOW COOKER:
6-quart

PREP TIME:
20 minutes

COOK TIME:
Low 5 to 6 hours

FINISHING COOK TIME:
High 10 to 15 minutes

Betty's Success Tip

If you happen to have any leftovers of this delicious turkey roast, remove the meat from the bones. Cut or slice the turkey into desired pieces. Wrap, seal securely, label and refrigerate up to 3 days or freeze up to 3 months. Thaw frozen turkey in the refrigerator before using.

Serving Suggestion

Fluffy homemade mashed potatoes are the perfect partner for this turkey breast. Leave the skins on or off—it's up to you.

2 tablespoons butter or margarine

1/2 cup chopped dried apricots

1/4 cup sweetened dried cranberries

1/4 cup real maple syrup

1/2 cup cream sherry or apple juice

2 tablespoons soy sauce

6- to 7-pound frozen bone-in whole turkey breast, thawed

1/2 teaspoon salt

1/8 teaspoon pepper

1/4 cup cornstarch

2 tablespoons water

4 medium green onions, sliced (1/4 cup)

1. Melt butter in 10-inch nonstick skillet over medium heat. Cook apricots and cranberries in butter 2 minutes, stirring occasionally. Stir in maple syrup, 1/4 cup of the sherry and the soy sauce. Cook 2 to 3 minutes, stirring occasionally, until mixture is reduced slightly. Cool 5 to 10 minutes. (Mixture will thicken slightly.)

2. Remove skin from turkey breast. Sprinkle turkey with salt and pepper. Place in 6-quart slow cooker. Spoon maple syrup mixture over turkey breast.

3. Cover and cook on low heat setting 5 to 6 hours or until juice of turkey is no longer pink when center is cut.

4. Remove turkey from cooker; cover to keep warm. Mix remaining 1/4 cup sherry, the cornstarch, water and onions; stir into mixture in cooker. Cover and cook on high heat setting 10 to 15 minutes or until mixture thickens slightly. Serve sauce with turkey.

1 Serving: Calories 535 (Calories from Fat 180); Fat 20g (Saturated 7g); Cholesterol 185mg; Sodium 540mg; Carbohydrate 21g (Dietary Fiber 1g); Protein 65g • **% Daily Value:** Vitamin A 16%; Vitamin C 2%; Calcium 4%; Iron 16% • **Diet Exchanges:** 8 Lean Meat, 1 Fruit, 1 Fat • **Carbohydrate Choices:** 1 1/2

Holiday Meals Made Easy

If you're looking for ways to make the holidays more carefree, put your slow cooker to work! You'll find that your slow cooker can free up your time, and when you're cooking for a crowd it can also free up oven space when you need it most. Let your slow cooker do the work for you so you can enjoy the holidays.

Get a Head Start

Relax and enjoy the festivities by preparing the basics a few days ahead.

- **Veggies:** Cut or chop vegetables such as carrots and onions; wrap them in plastic wrap or put in plastic containers and refrigerate. Keep bags of baby-cut carrots and frozen vegetables on hand for last-minute additions to your meal.
- **Seasonings:** Mix together herbs and spices and keep in a small bowl or plastic storage bag. Keep ready-to-use jars of minced garlic and canned chopped chilies on hand for extra flavor without extra chopping.
- **Liquids:** Measure out broth, juices or wine; cover and refrigerate.

- **Meats:** Stock your freezer with diced cooked chicken, cooked meatballs and ground beef and sausage so you can start an easy slow cooker dinner anytime during busy holidays.
- **Cheese:** Buy shredded cheese in lots of flavors to make easy, creamy dips to tide everyone over before dinner.
- **Sides:** Keep frozen rolls or biscuits on hand so you can pop them in the oven to heat while your slow cooker dinner finishes cooking.

Holiday Hints

Cook scrumptious sides, like stuffing, vegetables or potatoes in your slow cooker, or use it for the main course.

- **Cooked roasts and ham** should stand for 10 minutes before carving. This allows the juices to set up so the meat stays moist and is easier to carve.
- **Invite others to help.** Ask a family member or friend to prepare a recipe at home in their slow cooker and bring it for the meal. Or have someone bring a slow cooker appetizer for everyone to nibble on while you do the finishing touches to the meal.

- **Sweet potatoes or white potatoes?** Why not make both in your slow cooker? Make the Sweet Potatoes with Orange-Pecan Butter recipe on page 208 using half white potatoes and half sweet potatoes to please potato lovers of all kinds.
- **Borrow a slow cooker** from a friend or neighbor if you need another one.

Make It Special

An easy garnish or fun shape will make any slower cooker dish a little more special for the holidays.

- **Fresh rosemary sprigs** can be brushed with water and sprinkled with coarse salt for a "sparkling" garnish for a meat platter. Tuck in a few fresh cranberries for added color.
- **Butter pats** cut into holiday shapes add a festive touch for the breadbasket. Slice chilled butter 1/4 inch thick, and cut slices with mini heart or star-shaped cookie cutters. Use cutters with open tops so you can push the butter through. Place on waxed paper and refrigerate until serving time.

- **A fresh herb wreath** can decorate the top of a thick mixture such as a stew. Place sprigs of parsley, rosemary or thyme around the inside edge of the slow cooker. Make a bow using pimento strips to place on the wreath.
- **Mint sprigs and raspberries** can dress up a slow cooker dessert. Other options are lemon or orange zests, chopped crystallized ginger or a sprinkling of powdered sugar.

Holiday Menus

Warm up the holidays with these tasty slow cooker choices. To make it all easy when family and friends gather, start planning ahead and get all your shopping done in advance. Set the table and choose the serving pieces and decorations ahead of time, so there's no last-minute scrambling. You may want to borrow an extra slow cooker if you plan to make more than one of these delicious suggestions. And, don't be afraid to try a new dish or two. Who knows—this year's different dish may become next year's most requested!

Holiday	Appetizer	Salad/Veggie	Side Dish	Main Dish	Dessert
Thanksgiving	Maple-Mustard Barbecued Meatballs and Sausages (page 30)	Fresh Spinach Salad with Strawberries and Walnuts	Sweet Potatoes with Orange-Pecan Butter (page 208)	Glazed Oven Roasted Turkey	Pumpkin Pie
Christmas Eve	Party Crab Dip (page 16)	Roasted Brussels Sprouts, Parsnips, Carrots and Squash	Garlic-Parmesan Smashed Potatoes (page 204)	Swedish Meatballs (page 180)	Assorted Cookies and Bars
Christmas Day	Cheesy Chicken and Peppers Dip (page 18)	Caesar Salad	The Ultimate Creamed Corn (page 152)	Ham with Currant-Cherry Sauce (page 201)	French Silk Pie
New Year's Eve	Hot Artichoke and Spinach Dip (page 14)	Tossed Green Salad with Vinaigrette Dressing	Steamed Green Beans	Rosemary-Garlic Beef Roast (page 198)	Cherries Jubilee

Table Toppers

Looking for fast and festive decorations for your holiday table? These fuss-free ideas make celebrations a snap.

- **Large gold or silver doilies** at each place setting give an easy, elegant look. Place doilies underneath the dinner plates on the tablecloth or on each place mat. Sprinkle the table with gold confetti.
- **Candles** can bedeck the dining or buffet table with lots of glittering lights. Don't let a lack of candleholders stop you from lighting every nook and cranny. Hollow out a space in the center of apples just large enough to hold candles. Brush the insides of apples with lemon juice to prevent browning. Insert the candles, and wrap a rosemary sprig around the base of each apple.
- **A small memento** placed by each guest's place setting makes an evening memorable. It can be a small wrapped box with a single piece of premium candy to unwrap and eat at the end of the meal.
- **A basket or copper bowl** filled with small evergreen branches, pinecones, whole oranges and lemons, unshelled nuts and cinnamon sticks makes an easy seasonal centerpiece.

Bacon- and Corn Bread–Stuffed Turkey Breast

8 servings

SLOW COOKER:
5- to 6-quart

PREP TIME:
25 minutes

COOK TIME:
Low 7 to 8 hours

STAND TIME:
10 minutes

Betty's Success Tip

Although you normally remove the netting on a turkey before cooking, in this case leaving it on makes sense because it helps hold the turkey and stuffing together as they cook. Of course, you'll want to remove the netting before serving!

Serving Suggestion

Cooking your Thanksgiving turkey in a slow cooker allows you to spend more time with family and friends instead of being stuck in the kitchen for most of the day. For a traditional holiday meal, serve with cranberry sauce and sweet potatoes.

4 slices bacon, cut into 1/2-inch pieces

1 cup chopped red and green bell peppers

1 medium onion, chopped (1/2 cup)

1/2 cup frozen whole kernel corn

4 cups corn bread stuffing mix

1 teaspoon dried marjoram leaves

1/2 teaspoon seasoned salt

1/4 teaspoon pepper

1 1/2 cups water

3- to 4-pound frozen boneless whole turkey breast, thawed

1. Cook bacon in 12-inch skillet over medium heat, stirring occasionally, until brown. Stir in bell peppers, onion and corn. Cook 4 to 5 minutes, stirring occasionally, until vegetables are tender. Stir in stuffing mix, marjoram, seasoned salt, pepper and water until moistened.

2. Leave netting on turkey breast. Cut turkey breast (and netting) lengthwise in half from side without cutting completely through other side. Spoon and spread about 1 cup stuffing mixture onto turkey; fold turkey over filling. Tie 3 or 4 times with string (over netting) to hold together. Spray 5- to 6-quart slow cooker with cooking spray. Place stuffed turkey breast in cooker. Spoon remaining stuffing mixture around turkey.

3. Cover and cook on low heat setting 7 to 8 hours or until juice of turkey is no longer pink when center is cut. Remove turkey breast from cooker to serving platter; cover with foil. Let stand at room temperature 10 minutes before slicing. Remove string and netting before serving.

1 Serving: Calories 390 (Calories from Fat 110); Fat 12g (Saturated 4g); Cholesterol 100mg; Sodium 810mg; Carbohydrate 30g (Dietary Fiber 2g); Protein 40g • **% Daily Value:** Vitamin A 2%; Vitamin C 14%; Calcium 4%; Iron 14% • **Diet Exchanges:** 2 Starch, 4 1/2 Lean Meat • **Carbohydrate Choices:** 2

Bacon- and Corn Bread-Stuffed Turkey Breast

Provençal Beef with Zinfandel

12 servings

SLOW COOKER:
5- to 6-quart

PREP TIME:
25 minutes

COOK TIME:
Low 7 to 8 hours

FINISHING COOK TIME:
Low 20 to 30 minutes

Ingredient Substitution

Choose a hearty red Zinfandel or your favorite red wine for cooking this stew. If you prefer, you can use beef broth instead of the wine. To save time, you may want to use beef stew meat instead of cutting the beef roast into pieces.

Serving Suggestion

This flavorful, hearty stew tastes wonderful with egg noodles, but you might want to try something different. For a change serve with hot cooked barley, wild rice, brown rice or couscous.

6 slices bacon, cut into 1/2-inch pieces

3-pound beef boneless chuck roast, trimmed of fat and cut into 1-inch pieces

1 large onion, cut into 1/2-inch wedges

3 cups baby-cut carrots

1 cup red Zinfandel wine

3/4 cup beef broth

3 tablespoons all-purpose flour

1 teaspoon dried basil leaves

1/2 teaspoon dried thyme leaves

1/2 teaspoon salt

1/4 teaspoon pepper

1 can (14 1/2 ounces) diced tomatoes, undrained

1 package (8 ounces) sliced mushrooms

1/2 cup julienne-cut sun-dried tomatoes (not oil-packed)

Hot cooked egg noodles, if desired

Chopped fresh parsley or basil leaves, if desired

1. Cook bacon in 12-inch nonstick skillet over medium-high heat, stirring occasionally, until crisp. Place bacon in 5- to 6-quart slow cooker. Discard all but 1 tablespoon drippings in skillet. Cook beef in drippings in skillet 2 to 3 minutes, stirring occasionally, until brown. Stir onion into beef. Cook 1 minute, stirring occasionally. Spoon into cooker.

2. Stir remaining ingredients except mushrooms, sun-dried tomatoes, noodles and parsley into mixture in cooker.

3. Cover and cook on low heat setting 7 to 8 hours or until beef is tender.

4. Stir in mushrooms and sun-dried tomatoes. Cover and cook on low heat setting 20 to 30 minutes or until tender. Serve beef mixture over noodles; sprinkle with parsley.

1 Serving: Calories 280 (Calories from Fat 135); Fat 15g (Saturated 6g); Cholesterol 70mg; Sodium 380mg; Carbohydrate 10g (Dietary Fiber 2g); Protein 26g • **% Daily Value:** Vitamin A 100%; Vitamin C 8%; Calcium 2%; Iron 20% • **Diet Exchanges:** 3 Medium-Fat Meat, 2 Vegetable • **Carbohydrate Choices:** 1/2

Provençal Beef with Zinfandel

Rosemary-Garlic Beef Roast

12 servings

SLOW COOKER:
5- to 6-quart

PREP TIME:
15 minutes

COOK TIME:
Low 8 to 9 hours

FINISHING COOK TIME:
High 5 to 10 minutes

Ingredient Substitution

Out of chili sauce? In a pinch, ketchup will work. And if you have a hard time finding beef boneless sirloin tip at your supermarket, tri-tip will make a delicious roast.

Finishing Touch

For a festive holiday look, place the beef roast on a decorative platter and garnish with fresh rosemary sprigs and grape or cherry tomatoes.

1 tablespoon olive or vegetable oil

1 teaspoon Worcestershire sauce

5- to 6-pound beef boneless sirloin tip roast

2 cloves garlic, finely chopped

2 tablespoons chopped fresh rosemary leaves

1/2 teaspoon salt

1/2 teaspoon coarsely ground pepper

1 medium onion, sliced

1 cup beef broth

3 tablespoons chili sauce

1/3 cup all-purpose flour

1. Mix oil and Worcestershire sauce; brush over beef roast. Rub roast evenly with garlic, rosemary, salt and pepper. Place onion in 5- to 6-quart slow cooker; pour 1/4 cup of the broth over onion. Place beef roast on onion.

2. Cover and cook on low heat setting 8 to 9 hours or until beef is tender.

3. Remove beef from cooker; cover to keep warm. Mix remaining 3/4 cup broth, the chili sauce and flour in small bowl. Stir into hot mixture in cooker. Cook uncovered on high heat setting 5 to 10 minutes or until thickened. Serve gravy with beef.

1 Serving: Calories 240 (Calories from Fat 65); Fat 7g (Saturated 2g); Cholesterol 100mg; Sodium 310mg; Carbohydrate 5g (Dietary Fiber 0g); Protein 39g • **% Daily Value:** Vitamin A 2%; Vitamin C 0%; Calcium 0%; Iron 20% • **Diet Exchanges:** 5 1/2 Very Lean Meat, 1 Fat • **Carbohydrate Choices:** 0

Spinach- and Mushroom-Stuffed Pork Roast

6 servings

SLOW COOKER:
3 1/2- to 4-quart

PREP TIME:
30 minutes

COOK TIME:
Low 6 to 7 hours

Betty's Success Tip

If you don't have time to let the spinach thaw in the refrigerator, try running the package under cold water for a few minutes. Or thaw it in the microwave.

Serving Suggestion

Tired of the same old boiled or baked potatoes? For a change, try serving German spaetzle instead. Look for spaetzle in the frozen foods section of your supermarket.

2- to 2 1/2-pound pork boneless loin roast

2 tablespoons olive or vegetable oil

3 cloves garlic, finely chopped

1 package (6 ounces) fresh baby portabella mushrooms, chopped

1 package (9 ounces) frozen chopped spinach, thawed and squeezed to drain

1/2 cup soft bread crumbs (1 slice bread)

1/3 cup grated Parmesan cheese

1/2 teaspoon salt

1. To cut pork roast so that it can be filled and rolled, cut horizontally down length of pork about 1/2 inch from top of pork to within 3/4 inch of opposite side; open flat. Turn pork so you can cut other side. Repeat with other side of pork, cutting from the inside edge to the outer edge; open flat. If pork is thicker than 3/4 inch, cover pork with plastic wrap and pound until about 3/4-inch thickness. Remove plastic wrap.

2. Heat 1 tablespoon of the oil in 12-inch nonstick skillet over medium-high heat. Cook garlic and mushrooms in oil, stirring frequently, until liquid has evaporated. Stir in spinach, bread crumbs and cheese.

3. Spread mushroom mixture on inside surfaces of pork. Roll up pork; tie with kitchen twine. Heat remaining 1 tablespoon oil in 12-inch nonstick skillet over medium-high heat. Cook pork in oil until brown on all sides. Place pork in 3 1/2- to 4-quart slow cooker. Sprinkle with salt.

4. Cover and cook on low heat setting 6 to 7 hours or until pork is tender.

Cut horizontally down the length of the pork roast; open flat.   Cut horizontally from inside edge to outer edge; open flat.

1 Serving: Calories 360 (Calories from Fat 170); Fat 19g (Saturated 6g); Cholesterol 100mg; Sodium 460mg; Carbohydrate 10g (Dietary Fiber 2g); Protein 39g • **% Daily Value:** Vitamin A 54%; Vitamin C 4%; Calcium 14%; Iron 14% • **Diet Exchanges:** 5 Lean Meat, 2 Vegetable, 1 Fat • **Carbohydrate Choices:** 1/2

Spiced Orange Pork Roast

8 servings

SLOW COOKER:
3 1/2- to 4-quart

PREP TIME:
20 minutes

COOK TIME:
Low 9 to 11 hours

FINISHING COOK TIME:
15 minutes

Betty's Success Tip

To get the most juice from an orange, roll it around on a countertop a few times while applying gentle pressure before squeezing it.

Finishing Touch

Use an additional orange, cut into thin slices, as a garnish. Place the pork roast on a platter. Slit orange slices from the center through the outer rind, then twist and stand the orange twists all around the roast.

2 1/2- to 3-pound pork shoulder roast

1/2 teaspoon salt

1/4 teaspoon pepper

1 medium orange

1 bag (16 ounces) baby-cut carrots

1/2 cup dried apricots or orange-flavored dried plums

1/2 cup chicken broth

1/2 teaspoon ground cinnamon

1/4 teaspoon ground nutmeg

2 tablespoons cornstarch

1 tablespoon water

1 tablespoon honey

Chopped fresh parsley, if desired

1. Sprinkle pork with salt and pepper. Spray 10-inch skillet with cooking spray. Cook pork in skillet over medium-high heat until brown on all sides. Grate peel from orange; squeeze juice from orange. Reserve orange peel and juice.

2. Place pork in 3 1/2- to 4-quart slow cooker. Place carrots and apricots on pork. Mix broth, cinnamon, nutmeg and reserved orange peel and juice; pour over pork.

3. Cover and cook on low heat setting 9 to 11 hours or until pork is tender.

4. Remove pork, carrots and apricots from cooker; cover to keep warm. Skim fat from surface of juices in cooker; pour juices into 1-quart saucepan. Mix cornstarch and water until smooth; stir in honey. Stir honey mixture into juices in saucepan. Cook over medium-low heat about 15 minutes, stirring constantly, until mixture is smooth and bubbly. Serve pork with carrots, apricots and sauce. Sprinkle with parsley.

1 Serving: Calories 325 (Calories from Fat 155); Fat 17g (Saturated 6g); Cholesterol 90mg; Sodium 290mg; Carbohydrate 15g (Dietary Fiber 3g); Protein 31g • **% Daily Value:** Vitamin A 100%; Vitamin C 6%; Calcium 2%; Iron 10% • **Diet Exchanges:** 4 1/2 Lean Meat, 1 Fruit, 1/2 Fat • **Carbohydrate Choices:** 1

Ham with Currant-Cherry Sauce

12 servings

Photo on page 186

SLOW COOKER:
6-quart

PREP TIME:
20 minutes

COOK TIME:
Low 7 to 8 hours

Betty's Success Tip

Not sure what size ham to buy? Keep in mind that 1 pound of bone-in ham is enough for 2 servings.

Ingredient Substitution

A wide variety of dried fruits are now available at the supermarket. You could use dried blueberries, cherries or cranberries in place of the currants.

1 1/2 cups cherry preserves

1/4 cup balsamic vinegar

1/2 teaspoon ground mustard

1/2 teaspoon ground ginger

6- to 8-pound fully cooked bone-in ham

1/2 cup dried currants

2 teaspoons grated lemon peel

1 tablespoon chopped fresh chives

1. Mix preserves, vinegar, mustard and ginger in 2-cup glass measuring cup. Place ham in 6-quart slow cooker, trimming ham if necessary to fit. Brush ham with about 1/4 cup of the preserves mixture. Refrigerate remaining preserves mixture while ham cooks.

2. Cover and cook ham on low heat setting 7 to 8 hours.

3. About 20 minutes before ham is done, microwave remaining preserves mixture uncovered on High 4 minutes. Stir in currants and lemon peel; microwave uncovered on High about 3 minutes or until mixture just begins to boil. Stir in chives. Cool about 10 minutes.

4. Remove ham from cooker. Slice ham; place on serving platter. Serve sauce with ham.

1 Serving: Calories 280 (Calories from Fat 55); Fat 6g (Saturated 2g); Cholesterol 60mg; Sodium 1320mg; Carbohydrate 34g (Dietary Fiber 1g); Protein 23g • **% Daily Value:** Vitamin A 0%; Vitamin C 2%; Calcium 2%; Iron 10% • **Diet Exchanges:** 3 Very Lean Meat, 2 Fruit, 1 Fat • **Carbohydrate Choices:** 2

Apple-Walnut Stuffing

12 servings (about 3/4 cup each)

SLOW COOKER:
4- to 6-quart

PREP TIME:
20 minutes

COOK TIME:
Low 4 to 5 hours

Betty's Success Tip

Everyone loves stuffing! Cooking stuffing in its own dish instead of inside the bird will also produce moist and flavorful results. It's an easy solution that saves time since you don't have to remove the stuffing from the cooked bird when it's ready for carving.

Serving Suggestion

Stuffing is traditionally served with holiday turkey, but it's just as welcome with grilled chicken, pork roast or pork chops. So don't wait until the next holiday to serve this easy-to-make stuffing.

1/2 cup butter or margarine

1/2 cup chopped walnuts

1 tablespoon honey

1/8 teaspoon ground nutmeg

2 medium stalks celery, sliced (1 cup)

1 large onion, chopped (1 cup)

1 package (14 ounces) herb–seasoned stuffing cubes

1 jar (4 1/2 ounces) sliced mushrooms, drained

1 1/2 cups applesauce

2 cups water

1. Heat 2 tablespoons of the butter and the walnuts in 10-inch skillet over medium heat, stirring occasionally, until walnuts are lightly toasted. Remove walnuts from skillet, using slotted spoon; place in small dish. Stir honey and nutmeg into walnuts until glazed; set aside.

2. Melt remaining 6 tablespoons butter in same skillet over medium heat. Cook celery and onion in butter 3 to 4 minutes, stirring occasionally, until crisp-tender.

3. Spray 4- to 6-quart slow cooker with cooking spray. Place stuffing cubes in cooker. Add cooked celery and onion with butter and the mushrooms to stuffing cubes; mix lightly. Add applesauce and water; stir gently to mix.

4. Cover and cook on low heat setting 4 to 5 hours. Sprinkle with glazed walnuts before serving.

1 Serving: Calories 265 (Calories from Fat 110); Fat 12g (Saturated 5g); Cholesterol 20mg; Sodium 630mg; Carbohydrate 36g (Dietary Fiber 2g); Protein 5g • **% Daily Value:** Vitamin A 6%; Vitamin C 0%; Calcium 4%; Iron 8% • **Diet Exchanges:** 1 Starch, 1 Vegetable, 1 Fruit, 2 Fat • **Carbohydrate Choices:** 2 1/2

Pear-Apple Sauce with Cherries

15 servings (1/2 cup each)

SLOW COOKER:
3 1/2- to 4-quart

PREP TIME:
30 minutes

COOK TIME:
Low 7 to 8 hours

FINISHING COOK TIME:
High 15 to 30 minutes

Betty's Success Tip

After 7 hours in the slow cooker, the apples and the pears become quite tender and form a chunky-style sauce, even without mashing.

Serving Suggestion

This fruity sauce is wonderful when paired with the Bacon- and Corn Bread-Stuffed Turkey Breast (page 194). Because both require a slow cooker, make the Pear-Apple Sauce with Cherries the night before and serve it chilled with the turkey.

6 medium apples, peeled and chopped

6 medium pears, peeled and chopped

3/4 cup sugar

1/2 cup apple juice

3 teaspoons grated orange peel

1/4 teaspoon ground allspice

1 package (5 ounces) sweetened dried cherries (1 cup)

1. Mix apples, pears, sugar, apple juice, 2 teaspoons of the orange peel and the allspice in 3 1/2- to 4-quart slow cooker.

2. Cover and cook on low heat setting 7 to 8 hours or until fruit is tender.

3. Mash fruit with potato masher. Stir in remaining 1 teaspoon orange peel and the cherries. Cook uncovered on high heat setting 15 to 30 minutes or until desired consistency. Cool slightly. Serve warm or cool.

1 Serving: Calories 140 (Calories from Fat 0); Fat 0g (Saturated 0g); Cholesterol 0mg; Sodium 0mg; Carbohydrate 35g (Dietary Fiber 3g); Protein 0g • **% Daily Value:** Vitamin A 0%; Vitamin C 4%; Calcium 0%; Iron 0% • **Diet Exchanges:** 2 Fruit • **Carbohydrate Choices:** 2

Garlic-Parmesan Smashed Potatoes

12 servings

SLOW COOKER:
3 1/2- to 4-quart

PREP TIME:
20 minutes

COOK TIME:
High 4 to 6 hours

HOLD TIME:
Low up to 2 hours

Betty's Success Tip

You've read it right—these potatoes are smashed, not mashed—which means that there should be some lumps left. Both the lumps and potato skins add robust texture, which you don't get with regular mashed potatoes. If you don't have a potato masher on hand, using a large fork will do the trick.

Ingredient Substitution

If you want to trim a few calories during the holidays, use fat-free half-and-half in this recipe instead of regular half-and-half. No one will guess because the potatoes will still be rich and tasty.

8 medium unpeeled russet potatoes, cut into
  3/4- to 1-inch pieces (8 cups)

2 cloves garlic, finely chopped

1/4 cup butter or margarine

1/2 teaspoon salt

1/4 teaspoon pepper

1 cup water

1/2 cup half-and-half

3/4 cup shredded Parmesan cheese

1/4 cup chopped fresh basil leaves

1. Place potatoes in 3 1/2- to 4-quart slow cooker. Stir in garlic, butter, salt, pepper and water.

2. Cover and cook on high heat setting 4 to 6 hours or until potatoes are tender.

3. Do not drain potatoes. Mash potatoes slightly with potato masher. Add half-and-half and cheese; continue mashing until desired consistency and some lumps remain. Stir in basil just before serving. Potatoes will hold on low heat setting up to 2 hours.

1 Serving: Calories 165 (Calories from Fat 65); Fat 7g (Saturated 4g); Cholesterol 20mg; Sodium 250mg; Carbohydrate 21g (Dietary Fiber 2g); Protein 5g • **% Daily Value:** Vitamin A 6%; Vitamin C 8%; Calcium 10%; Iron 6% • **Diet Exchanges:** 1 1/2 Starch, 1 Fat • **Carbohydrate Choices:** 1 1/2

Garlic-Parmesan Smashed Potatoes

Creamed Potatoes with Garden Peas

10 servings (1/2 cup each)

SLOW COOKER:
3 1/2- to 4-quart

PREP TIME:
10 minutes

COOK TIME:
High 3 to 4 hours

FINISHING COOK TIME:
High 20 to 30 minutes

Betty's Success Tip

The peas are added at the end so they maintain their texture and bright green color. If you don't have 30 minutes for them to warm through, just cook the peas separately in the microwave and stir in.

Finishing Touch

To make this luscious side dish even more appealing, sprinkle chopped fresh chives or chopped fresh or dried dill weed on top before serving.

2 pounds small red potatoes (2 to 3 inches in diameter), cut into 1/4-inch slices (8 cups)

4 medium green onions, sliced (1/4 cup)

2 cloves garlic, finely chopped

1 container (10 ounces) refrigerated Alfredo pasta sauce

1/2 cup half-and-half or milk

1/2 teaspoon salt

1/8 teaspoon pepper

1 1/2 cups frozen green peas (from 1-pound bag)

1. Spray 3 1/2- to 4-quart slow cooker with cooking spray. Layer half each of the potatoes, onions and garlic in cooker. Mix pasta sauce, half-and-half, salt and pepper; spoon half of mixture over potatoes and onions. Layer with remaining potatoes, onions, garlic and sauce mixture. Do not stir.

2. Cover and cook on high heat setting 3 to 4 hours.

3. About 30 minutes before serving, sprinkle peas over potato mixture. Cover and cook on high heat setting 20 to 30 minutes or until peas are hot. Stir gently before serving.

1 Serving: Calories 215 (Calories from Fat 100); Fat 11g (Saturated 7g); Cholesterol 30mg; Sodium 270mg; Carbohydrate 24g (Dietary Fiber 3g); Protein 5g • **% Daily Value:** Vitamin A 10%; Vitamin C 10%; Calcium 10%; Iron 8% • **Diet Exchanges:** 1 1/2 Starch, 2 Fat • **Carbohydrate Choices:** 1 1/2

Smoky Cheese and Potato Bake

14 servings (1/2 cup each)

SLOW COOKER:
3 1/2- to 4-quart

PREP TIME:
10 minutes

COOK TIME:
Low 5 to 6 hours

Betty's Success Tip

If curiosity is getting the better of you, and you want to see what's happening to the food in your slow cooker, don't give in! Just spin the slow cooker lid to dissipate the moisture rather than lifting it. You add time to the cooking process every time you lift the lid.

Ingredient Substitution

Vary the taste by using whatever creamed soup you have on hand, such as cream of onion, chicken or broccoli.

1 can (10 3/4 ounces) condensed cream of mushroom soup

1 container (8 ounces) sour cream (1 cup)

1 round (7 ounces) hickory-smoked Gouda cheese, cut into 1/2-inch cubes

1/3 cup drained roasted red bell pepper strips (from 7-ounce jar)

1 bag (32 ounces) frozen southern-style cubed hash brown potatoes (8 cups), thawed

2 tablespoons chopped fresh chives

1. Spray 3 1/2- to 4-quart slow cooker with cooking spray. Mix soup, sour cream and cheese in medium bowl. Gently stir in bell pepper strips.

2. Arrange half of the potatoes in cooker. Top with half of the sour cream mixture; spread evenly. Top with remaining potatoes and sour cream mixture, spreading evenly. Do not stir.

3. Cover and cook on low heat setting 5 to 6 hours. Sprinkle chives over potatoes before serving.

1 Serving: Calories 180 (Calories from Fat 70); Fat 8g (Saturated 5g); Cholesterol 25mg; Sodium 320mg; Carbohydrate 21g (Dietary Fiber 1g); Protein 6g • **% Daily Value:** Vitamin A 8%; Vitamin C 10%; Calcium 14%; Iron 2% • **Diet Exchanges:** 1 1/2 Starch, 1/2 High-Fat Meat, 1 Fat • **Carbohydrate Choices:** 1 1/2

Sweet Potatoes
with Orange-Pecan Butter

12 servings

SLOW COOKER:
5- to 6-quart

PREP TIME:
10 minutes

COOK TIME:
Low 7 to 8 hours

12 unpeeled dark-orange sweet potatoes (6 to 8 ounces each)

2 tablespoons butter or margarine, melted

1 teaspoon seasoned salt

1/2 teaspoon coarsely ground pepper

Orange-Pecan Butter (below)

Ingredient Substitution

If there's someone in your family who's not a fan of sweet potatoes, prepare this updated classic using half russet potatoes and half sweet potatoes instead.

1. Pierce sweet potatoes with fork. Brush each potato with melted butter. Sprinkle with seasoned salt and pepper. Wrap potatoes individually in aluminum foil. Place in 5- to 6-quart slow cooker.

2. Cover and cook on low heat setting 7 to 8 hours or until potatoes are tender.

3. Meanwhile, make Orange-Pecan Butter.

4. Remove potatoes from cooker; remove foil. Serve potatoes with Orange-Pecan Butter.

Finishing Touch

The Orange-Pecan Butter can be pressed into a 1-cup mold that has been lined with plastic wrap. Cover with plastic wrap and refrigerate 2 hours or until firm. Unmold the butter onto a small serving plate.

Orange-Pecan Butter

1/2 cup chopped pecans

1/2 cup butter or margarine, softened

1/4 cup orange marmalade

1 tablespoon cream sherry, if desired

Heat oven to 375°. Place pecans in shallow baking pan. Bake 4 to 6 minutes or until toasted; cool slightly. Mix butter, marmalade, sherry and pecans in small bowl. Spoon into decorative serving bowl. Serve butter at room temperature. Store in refrigerator.

1 Serving: Calories 250 (Calories from Fat 110); Fat 12g (Saturated 6g); Cholesterol 25mg; Sodium 130mg; Carbohydrate 33g (Dietary Fiber 4g); Protein 3g • **% Daily Value:** Vitamin A 100%; Vitamin C 24%; Calcium 4%; Iron 4% • **Diet Exchanges:** 1 Starch, 1 Fruit, 2 1/2 Fat • **Carbohydrate Choices:** 2

Sweet Potatoes with Orange-Pecan Butter

Honey-Cranberry Butternut Squash

6 servings

SLOW COOKER:
6-quart

PREP TIME:
20 minutes

COOK TIME:
Low 5 to 6 hours

Betty's Success Tip

Butternut squash has the same shape as a lightbulb or pear—it's wider at one end than the other. It usually weighs between 2 and 3 pounds, and its shell is golden yellow to camel colored.

Serving Suggestion

When served with turkey and wild rice, this squash makes a satisfying and flavorful holiday meal. Add a fresh sliced orange and onion salad on Bibb lettuce, drizzled with raspberry vinaigrette. End the meal with parfait glasses filled with peppermint ice cream and hot fudge sauce, topped with a fresh mint leaf.

3 medium butternut squash (6 to 7 inches long)

1/3 cup frozen (thawed) cranberry-apple juice concentrate

1/3 cup honey

2 tablespoons butter or margarine, melted

3/4 cup sweetened dried cranberries

3 tablespoons chopped crystallized ginger

1/4 teaspoon salt

1/4 cup water

1/4 cup chopped walnuts

1. Cut each squash lengthwise in half; remove seeds. Mix juice concentrate, honey and butter in small bowl. Stir in cranberries and 2 tablespoons of the ginger. Spoon mixture evenly into each squash cavity; sprinkle with salt. Layer squash in 6-quart slow cooker. Carefully pour water into bottom of cooker.

2. Cover and cook on low heat setting 5 to 6 hours or until tender. Sprinkle walnuts and remaining 1 tablespoon ginger over squash halves.

1 Serving: Calories 300 (Calories from Fat 63); Fat 7g (Saturated 3g); Cholesterol 10mg; Sodium 135mg; Carbohydrate 57g (Dietary Fiber 4g); Protein 3g • **% Daily Value:** Vitamin A 100%; Vitamin C 32%; Calcium 8%; Iron 8% • **Diet Exchanges:** 1 Starch, 3 Fruit, 1 Fat • **Carbohydrate Choices:** 4

Southwest Vegetable Stew

10 servings (about 1 1/2 cups each)

SLOW COOKER:
6-quart

PREP TIME:
30 minutes

COOK TIME:
Low 5 to 6 hours

Betty's Success Tip

Pretty much anything goes in this recipe, so feel free to add your favorite beans and root vegetables. You may want to try garbanzo beans, whole green beans or sliced turnips or rutabaga.

Finishing Touch

Instead of sprinkling this hearty meatless stew with cilantro, you can top it with fresh chives or shredded or shavings of Parmesan cheese.

3 medium dark-orange sweet potatoes, peeled and cut into 1-inch pieces (4 cups)

8 small unpeeled red potatoes, cut into 1-inch pieces (4 cups)

4 medium carrots, cut into 1/2-inch pieces (3 cups)

2 medium parsnips, peeled and cut into 1/2-inch pieces (2 1/2 cups)

1 medium green bell pepper, cut into 1/2-inch pieces (1 1/2 cups)

1 medium onion, cut into 1/2-inch wedges (1 cup)

2 cloves garlic, finely chopped

2 cans (14 1/2 ounces each) stewed tomatoes, undrained

1/4 cup tomato paste

1 1/2 teaspoons dried oregano leaves

1 1/2 teaspoons ground cumin

1 teaspoon salt

1/4 teaspoon pepper

1/4 cup chopped fresh cilantro

1. Mix all ingredients except cilantro in 6-quart slow cooker.

2. Cover and cook on low heat setting 5 to 6 hours or until vegetables are tender. Spoon into shallow serving bowls; sprinkle with cilantro.

1 Serving: Calories 210 (Calories from Fat 0); Fat 0g (Saturated 0g); Cholesterol 0mg; Sodium 540mg; Carbohydrate 55g (Dietary Fiber 7g); Protein 5g • **% Daily Value:** Vitamin A 100%; Vitamin C 50%; Calcium 8%; Iron 12% • **Diet Exchanges:** 1 Starch, 2 1/2 Fruit • **Carbohydrate Choices:** 3 1/2

Helpful Nutrition
and Cooking Information

Nutrition Guidelines

We provide nutrition information for each recipe that includes calories, fat, cholesterol, sodium, carbohydrate, fiber and protein. Individual food choices can be based on this information.

Recommended intake for a daily diet of 2,000 calories as set by the Food and Drug Administration

Total Fat	Less than 65g
Saturated Fat	Less than 20g
Cholesterol	Less than 300mg
Sodium	Less than 2,400mg
Total Carbohydrate	300g
Dietary Fiber	25g

Criteria Used for Calculating Nutrition Information

- The first ingredient was used wherever a choice is given (such as 1/3 cup sour cream or plain yogurt).

- The first ingredient amount was used wherever a range is given (such as 3- to 3-1/2-pound cut-up broiler-fryer chicken).

- The first serving number was used wherever a range is given (such as 4 to 6 servings).

- "If desired" ingredients and recipe variations were not included (such as sprinkle with brown sugar, if desired).

- Only the amount of a marinade or frying oil that is estimated to be absorbed by the food during preparation or cooking was calculated.

Ingredients Used in Recipe Testing and Nutrition Calculations

- Ingredients used for testing represent those that the majority of consumers use in their homes: large eggs, 2% milk, 80%-lean ground beef, canned ready-to-use chicken broth and vegetable oil spread containing not less than 65 percent fat.

- Fat-free, low-fat or low-sodium products were not used, unless otherwise indicated.

- Solid vegetable shortening (not butter, margarine, nonstick cooking sprays or vegetable oil spread as they can cause sticking problems) was used to grease pans, unless otherwise indicated.

Equipment Used in Recipe Testing

We use equipment for testing that the majority of consumers use in their homes. If a specific piece of equipment (such as a wire whisk) is necessary for recipe success, it is listed in the recipe.

- Cookware and bakeware without nonstick coatings were used, unless otherwise indicated.

- No dark-colored, black or insulated bakeware was used.

- When a pan is specified in a recipe, a metal pan was used; a baking dish or pie plate means ovenproof glass was used.

- An electric hand mixer was used for mixing only when mixer speeds are specified in the recipe directions. When a mixer speed is not given, a spoon or fork was used.

Cooking Terms Glossary

Beat: Mix ingredients vigorously with spoon, fork, wire whisk, hand beater or electric mixer until smooth and uniform.

Boil: Heat liquid until bubbles rise continuously and break on the surface and steam is given off. For rolling boil, the bubbles form rapidly.

Chop: Cut into coarse or fine irregular pieces with a knife, food chopper, blender or food processor.

Cube: Cut into squares 1/2 inch or larger.

Dice: Cut into squares smaller than 1/2 inch.

Grate: Cut into tiny particles using small rough holes of grater (citrus peel or chocolate).

Grease: Rub the inside surface of a pan with shortening, using pastry brush, piece of waxed paper or paper towel, to prevent food from sticking during baking (as for some casseroles).

Julienne: Cut into thin, matchlike strips, using knife or food processor (vegetables, fruits, meats).

Mix: Combine ingredients in any way that distributes them evenly.

Sauté: Cook foods in hot oil or margarine over medium-high heat with frequent tossing and turning motion.

Shred: Cut into long thin pieces by rubbing food across the holes of a shredder, as for cheese, or by using a knife to slice very thinly, as for cabbage.

Simmer: Cook in liquid just below the boiling point on top of the stove; usually after reducing heat from a boil. Bubbles will rise slowly and break just below the surface.

Stir: Mix ingredients until uniform consistency. Stir once in a while for stirring occasionally, often for stirring frequently and continuously for stirring constantly.

Toss: Tumble ingredients (such as green salad) lightly with a lifting motion, usually to coat evenly or mix with another food.

Metric Conversion Guide

Volume

U.S. Units	Canadian Metric	Australian Metric
1/4 teaspoon	1 mL	1 ml
1/2 teaspoon	2 mL	2 ml
1 teaspoon	5 mL	5 ml
1 tablespoon	15 mL	20 ml
1/4 cup	50 mL	60 ml
1/3 cup	75 mL	80 ml
1/2 cup	125 mL	125 ml
2/3 cup	150 mL	170 ml
3/4 cup	175 mL	190 ml
1 cup	250 mL	250 ml
1 quart	1 liter	1 liter
1 1/2 quarts	1.5 liters	1.5 liters
2 quarts	2 liters	2 liters
2 1/2 quarts	2.5 liters	2.5 liters
3 quarts	3 liters	3 liters
4 quarts	4 liters	4 liters

Weight

U.S. Units	Canadian Metric	Australian Metric
1 ounce	30 grams	30 grams
2 ounces	55 grams	60 grams
3 ounces	85 grams	90 grams
4 ounces (1/4 pound)	115 grams	125 grams
8 ounces (1/2 pound)	225 grams	225 grams
16 ounces (1 pound)	455 grams	500 grams
1 pound	455 grams	1/2 kilogram

Measurements

Inches	Centimeters
1	2.5
2	5.0
3	7.5
4	10.0
5	12.5
6	15.0
7	17.5
8	20.5
9	23.0
10	25.5
11	28.0
12	30.5
13	33.0

Temperatures

Fahrenheit	Celsius
32°	0°
212°	100°
250°	120°
275°	140°
300°	150°
325°	160°
350°	180°
375°	190°
400°	200°
425°	220°
450°	230°
475°	240°
500°	260°

Note: The recipes in this cookbook have not been developed or tested using metric measures. When converting recipes to metric, some variations in quality may be noted.

Index

Numbers in **_bold italics_** indicate photos.

A

Alfredo, holiday chicken, 188, _189_
Alfredo pasta sauce, in Creamed Potatoes with Garden Peas, 206
Almonds. _See_ Nuts
Appetizers
  Asian Chicken Drummies, _10_, 23
  French Onion Meatballs, 28, _29_
  Hot and Spicy Riblets, 31
  Hot Dog and Bacon Roll-Ups, 25
  Maple-Mustard Barbecued Meatballs and Sausages, 30
  Mini Cheeseburger Bites, 26, _27_
  Teriyaki Smoked Riblets, 32, _33_
  White Chili Mini Tacos, 24
Apple(s)
  pear-, sauce with cherries, 203
  -Walnut Stuffing, 202
Applesauce, in
  Apple-Walnut Stuffing, 202
  Chicken–Wild Rice Casserole with Dried Cherries, 69
Apricots, in
  Apricot-Glazed Pork Roast and Stuffing, 84, _85_
  Maple- and Apricot-Sauced Turkey Breast, 191
  Spiced Orange Pork Roast, 200
Artichoke and spinach dip, hot, 14, _15_
Asian BBQ Beef Brisket, 106
Asian Chicken Drummies, _10_, 23
Asian Hoisin Ribs, 82, _83_
Asian Meatballs, 178, _179_
Asparagus
  beef and, over noodles, 104
  ham and, chowder, 129
  with mustard, 71
Avocados, in Make-Your-Own Taco Salad, 176

B

Bacon
  Bacon- and Corn Bread–Stuffed Turkey Breast, 194, _195_
  in Easy Savory Baked Beans, 136
  Hot Dog and Bacon Roll-Ups, 25
  in Provençal Beef with Zinfandel, 196, _197_
  Smoky Bacon and Gruyère Dip, 13
  in Texas-Style Barbecued Beans, 181
Bagel chips, in Chex Party Mix, 34
Bake, turkey sausage–bean, 74
Baked beans
  easy savory, 136
  southwestern calico, 182
  sweet maple, _130_, 132
Baked Potato Bar, 183
Barbecued beans, Texas-style, 181
Barbecued Beef and Pork Sandwiches, 163
Barbecued beef brisket, Asian, 106
Barbecued chicken sandwiches, teriyaki, 160, _161_
Barbecued meatballs and sausages, maple-mustard, 30
Barbecued Pork Chops, 122, _123_
Barley Casserole with Peas and Peppers, 140, _141_
Barley-Vegetable Soup, 38
Bayou Gumbo, _36_, 46
BBQ beef brisket, Asian, 106
Beans. _See also_ Chili
  baked, in Easy Savory Baked Beans, 136
  baked, southwestern calico, 182
  black, Caribbean Black Beans, 138
  black, in Black Bean and Corn Salad, 71
  black, in Hot Nacho Bean Dip, 12
  black, in Mexican Beef Stew, 54, _55_
  black, in Spicy Black Bean Barbecue Chili, 64, 65
  black, in Texas-Style Barbecued Beans, 181
  cannellini, in Chicken and Bean Tacos, 162
  cannellini, in Chicken and Vegetable Tortellini Stew, 50, _51_

cannellini, in White Chili Mini Tacos, 24
chili, in Crowd-Pleasing Chili, 172
finishing touches for, 107
garbanzo, in Green Chile and Pork Stew, 86
garbanzo, in Two-Bean Minestrone, 42
great northern, in Country French White Beans, 134, _135_
great northern, in Garlic Chicken with Italian Beans, 98, _99_
great northern, in Pork Tortilla Soup, 47
great northern, in Texas-Style Barbecued Beans, 181
great northern, in Turkey Sausage–Bean Bake, 74
great northern, in White Chili with Chicken, 61
green, in Barley-Vegetable Soup, 38
green, in Beef and Creamy Potato Casserole, 116
green, in Hunter's-Style Pork Roast, 117
green, in Southern-Style String Beans, 146, _147_
green, in Vegetable Beef Stew, 60
kidney, in Crowd-Pleasing Chili, 172
kidney, in Mexican Beef Chili, 63
kidney, in Southwestern Calico Baked Beans, 182
kidney, New Orleans–style, 139
lima, in Southwestern Calico Baked Beans, 182
navy, in Sweet Maple Baked Beans, _130_, 132
navy, Smoky Ham and Navy Bean Stew, 49
pinto, in Make-Your-Own Taco Salad, 176
pinto, in Southwestern Pinto Beans, 133
pinto, in Turkey Chili, _158_, 171
refried, in Beef and Green Chile Tortilla Dinner, 177
refried, in Hot Nacho Bean Dip, 12

Beef recipes
  Asian BBQ Beef Brisket, 106
  Asian Meatballs, 178, *179*
  Barbecued Beef and Pork
    Sandwiches, 163
  Beef and Asparagus Over Noodles,
    104
  Beef and Creamy Potato Casserole,
    116
  Beef and Green Chile Tortilla
    Dinner, 177
  Beef au Jus Sandwiches, 166, *167*
  Beef Carbonnade with Potatoes,
    76, *77*
  Beef Pot Roast with Vegetables, 78
  Beef Roast with Shiitake
    Mushroom Sauce, 102, *103*
  Cheesy Ravioli Casserole, 184, *185*
  Chinese Beef and Broccoli, 105
  Corned Beef Brisket with
    Horseradish Sour Cream, 79
  Crowd-Pleasing Chili, 172
  French Onion Meatballs, 28, *29*
  Hamburger Hash, 173
  Italian Meatballs with Marinara
    Sauce, 114, *115*
  Make-Your-Own Taco Salad, 176
  Maple-Mustard Barbecued
    Meatballs and Sausages, 30
  Meatball Stone Soup, 44, *45*
  Mexican Beef Chili, 63
  Mexican Beef Stew, 54, *55*
  Mini Cheeseburger Bites, 26, *27*
  Pizza Joe Sandwiches, 170
  Pot Roast–Style Beef Steak, 110, *111*
  Provençal Beef with Zinfandel,
    196, *197*
  Rosemary-Garlic Beef Roast, 198
  Savory Beef Short Rib Dinner,
    92, 112
  Slow-Simmered Spaghetti Meat
    Sauce, 113
  Swedish Meatballs, 180
  Vegetable Beef Stew, 60
  Zesty Italian Beef Tips, 80
Beer, in Beef Carbonnade with
    Potatoes, 76, *77*
Beets, orange-glazed, 148
Berries. *See specific types*

Biscuits
  butter, 43
  French onion, quick, 43
Bisquick, dishes with
  Butter Biscuits, 43
  Quick Corn Bread Sticks, 43
  Quick French Onion Biscuits, 43
  Triple-Cheese Flatbread, 43
Black beans. *See* Beans, black
Black-eyed peas. *See* Peas, black-eyed
Brazilian Saffron Chicken and Rice,
    96, *97*
Breads
  easy homemade, 43
  on the side, 43
  sticks, corn, quick, 43
Brisket
  beef, Asian BBQ, 106
  corned beef, and cabbage dinner,
    108, *109*
  corned beef, with horseradish sour
    cream, 79
Broccoli
  Chinese beef and, 105
  Holiday Chicken Alfredo, 188, *189*
  Spicy Pork and Pineapple Salad, 121
Brown Sugar Strawberries, 71
Buffet basics, 17
Burgers. *See also* Hamburger Hash
  Mini Cheeseburger Bites, 26, *27*
Burritos, southwestern pork, 168, *169*
Butter, orange-pecan, 208, *209*
Butter Biscuits, 43
Butternut squash, honey-cranberry,
    210

C
Cabbage
  corned beef and, dinner, 108, *109*
  in Harvest Sausage-Vegetable
    Casserole, 75
Caesar Vegetable Medley, 71
Candied Sweet Potatoes, *127*, 155
Carbonnade, beef, with potatoes,
    76, *77*
Caribbean Black Beans, 138
Carrots, in
  Barley-Vegetable Soup, 38
  Beef Pot Roast with Vegetables, 78

Black-Eyed Pea and Sausage
    Soup, 48
Chicken and Vegetable Tortellini
    Stew, 50, *51*
Chicken Stew, *66*, 68
Chicken–Wild Rice Casserole with
    Dried Cherries, 69
Corned Beef and Cabbage Dinner,
    108, *109*
Creamy Chicken and Wild Rice
    Soup, 39
Fisherman's Wharf Seafood Stew,
    52, *53*
Ham and Lentil Stew, 90, *91*
Hamburger Hash, 173
Harvest Sausage-Vegetable
    Casserole, 75
Hunter's-Style Pork Roast, 117
Lentils and Veggies, 144
Pineapple Carrots, 149
Pot Roast–Style Beef Steak, 110, *111*
Provençal Beef with Zinfandel,
    196, *197*
Savory Beef Short Rib Dinner,
    92, 112
Scottish Lamb Stew, 56, *57*
Slow-Simmered Spaghetti Meat
    Sauce, 113
Smoky Ham and Navy Bean Stew, 49
Southwestern Pinto Beans, 133
Southwest Vegetable Stew, 211
Spiced Orange Pork Roast, 200
Sweet-and-Sour Chicken, 94, *95*
Turkey Sausage–Bean Bake, 74
Vegetable Beef Stew, 60
Cashews. *See* Nuts
Casserole dishes
  Barley Casserole with Peas and
    Peppers, 140, *141*
  Beef and Creamy Potato Casserole,
    116
  Cheesy Ravioli Casserole, 184, *185*
  Chicken–Wild Rice Casserole with
    Dried Cherries, 69
  finishing touches for, 107
  Harvest Sausage-Vegetable
    Casserole, 75
  Sour Cream and Onion Potato
    Casserole, 154

Cauliflower, in
    Cauliflower Curry, 150, *151*
    Curried Pork Stew, 58, *59*
Celebrate summer, 137
Celery, in
    Apple-Walnut Stuffing, 202
    Barley-Vegetable Soup, 38
    Beef Pot Roast with Vegetables, 78
    Chicken and Sausage Jambalaya,
        174, *175*
    Chicken–Wild Rice Casserole with
        Dried Cherries, 69
    Ham and Lentil Stew 90, *91*
    New Orleans–Style Red Beans, 139
    Smoky Ham and Navy Bean Stew, 49
    soup, in Ham with Cheesy Potatoes,
        88, *89*
    Southwestern Pinto Beans, 133
    Turkey Breast with Sherried
        Stuffing, 70
    Vegetable Beef Stew, 60
Cereal, in Chex Party Mix, 34
Cheese. *See also* Cream cheese
    American, in Make-Your-Own Taco
        Salad, 176
    American, in Mini Cheeseburger
        Bites, 26, *27*
    American, in Sour Cream and
        Onion Potato Casserole, 154
    Cheddar, in Cheesy Chicken and
        Peppers Dip, 18, *19*
    Cheddar, in Ham with Cheesy
        Potatoes, 88, *89*
    Cheddar, in Make-Your-Own Taco
        Salad, 176
    Cheddar, in Sour Cream and Onion
        Potato Casserole, 154
    Cheddar, in Supper Ham Frittata,
        128
    Cheddar, in Triple-Cheese
        Flatbread, 43
    feta, in Greek-Style Veggies, 153
    Gouda, in Smoky Cheese and
        Potato Bake, 207
    Gruyère, in smoky bacon and, dip, 13
    Mexican cheese blend, in Beef and
        Green Chile Tortilla Dinner, 177
    Mexican cheese blend, in Hot
        Nacho Bean Dip, 12

Monterey Jack, in Cheesy Pork
    Quesadillas, 120
Monterey Jack, in Ham with
    Cheesy Potatoes, 88, *89*
Monterey Jack, in Triple-Cheese
    Flatbread, 43
mozzarella, in Cheesy Ravioli
    Casserole, 184, *185*
mozzarella, in Pizza Fondue, 20, *21*
mozzarella, in Pizza Joe Sandwiches,
    170
mozzarella, in Sausage and
    Pepperoni Dip, 22
Parmesan, garlic-, smashed potatoes,
    125, 204, *205*
Parmesan, in Holiday Chicken
    Alfredo, 188, *189*
Parmesan, in Spinach- and
    Mushroom-Stuffed Pork Roast,
    199
Parmesan, in Triple-Cheese
    Flatbread, 43
provolone, in Beef au Jus
    Sandwiches, 166, *167*
Swiss, in Hot Artichoke and
    Spinach Dip, 14, *15*
triple-, flatbread, 43
Cheeseburger bites, mini, 26, *27*
Cheesy Chicken and Peppers Dip, 18, *19*
Cheesy Pork Quesadillas, 120
Cheesy Ravioli Casserole, 184, *185*
Cherry(ies)
    currant-, sauce, ham with, *186*, 201
    dried, chicken–wild rice casserole
        with, 69
    pear-apple sauce with, 203
Chex Party Mix, 34
Chicken, finishing touches for, 107
Chicken recipes
    Asian Chicken Drummies, *10*, 23
    Brazilian Saffron Chicken and Rice,
        96, *97*
    Cheesy Chicken and Peppers Dip,
        18, *19*
    Chicken and Bean Tacos, 162
    Chicken and Sausage Jambalaya,
        174, *175*
    Chicken and Vegetable Tortellini
        Stew, 50, *51*

Chicken Breasts with Mushroom
    Cream Sauce, 190
Chicken Stew, *66*, 68
Chicken–Wild Rice Casserole with
    Dried Cherries, 69
Chunky Chicken Chili with
    Hominy, 62
Creamy Chicken and Wild Rice
    Soup, 39
Garlic Chicken with Italian Beans,
    98, *99*
Harvest Sausage-Vegetable
    Casserole, 75
Holiday Chicken Alfredo, 188, *189*
Spicy Chicken in Peanut Sauce, 100
Sweet-and-Sour Chicken, 94, *95*
Teriyaki Barbecued Chicken
    Sandwiches, 160, *161*
White Chili Mini Tacos, 24
White Chili with Chicken, 61
Chiles/chilies
    chipotle, in Asian BBQ Beef
        Brisket, 106
    chipotle, in Mexican Pork Roast
        with Chili Sauce, 118, *119*
    chipotle, in Southwestern Pinto
        Beans, 133
    chipotle, in Hot and Spicy Riblets, 31
    chipotle, in Spicy Black Bean
        Barbecue Chili, 64, *65*
    finishing touches for, 107
    green, in Beef and Green Chile
        Tortilla Dinner, 177
    green, in Cheesy Chicken and
        Peppers Dip, 18, *19*
    green, in Chicken and Bean Tacos,
        162
    green, in Green Chile and Pork
        Stew, 86
    green, in Hot Nacho Bean Dip, 12
    green, in Turkey Chili, *158*, 171
    green, in White Chili Mini Tacos, 24
    green, in White Chili with
        Chicken, 61
Chili. *See also* Stews
    Chunky Chicken Chili with
        Hominy, 62
    Crowd-Pleasing Chili, 172
    Mexican Beef Chili, 63

Chili *(cont.)*
  Spicy Black Bean Barbecue Chili,
    64, 65
  Turkey Chili, *158*, 171
  White Chili with Chicken, 61
Chinese Beef and Broccoli, 105
Chipotle chilies. *See* Chiles/chilies
Chocolate, honey-, sundaes, 71
Chowder, ham and asparagus, 129
Chunky Chicken Chili with
    Hominy, 62
Chutney, fruit, ham with, 87
Cocktail sausages, in Maple-Mustard
    Barbecued Meatballs and
    Sausages, 30
Coconut milk, in Cauliflower Curry,
    150, *151*
Cod, in Fisherman's Wharf Seafood
    Stew, 52, *53*
Cola, in Savory Barbecued Ribs,
    124, *125*
Coleslaw mix, in Teriyaki Barbecued
    Chicken Sandwiches, 160, *161*
Corn
  in Bacon- and Corn Bread–Stuffed
    Turkey Breast, 194, *195*
  in Barley-Vegetable Soup, 38
  black bean and, salad, 71
  creamed, ultimate, 152
  in Mexican Beef Stew, 54, *55*
  in Vegetable Beef Stew, 60
Corn bread–, and bread-stuffed
    turkey breast, 194, *195*
Corn bread sticks, quick, 43
Corn chips, in Make-Your-Own Taco
    Salad, 176
Corned Beef and Cabbage Dinner,
    108, *109*
Corned Beef Brisket with
    Horseradish Sour Cream, 79
Cornmeal, in Turkey Chili, *158*, 171
Country French White Beans, 134, *135*
Country-Style Ribs and Sauerkraut, 81
Couscous, in Spicy Chicken in
    Peanut Sauce, 100
Crab dip, party, 16
Cranberry(ies)
  Maple- and Apricot-Sauced Turkey
    Breast, 191

Honey-Cranberry Butternut
    Squash, 210
Cream cheese, in
  Cheesy Chicken and Peppers Dip,
    18, *19*
  Party Crab Dip, 16
  Pizza Fondue, 20, *21*
  Smoky Bacon and Gruyère Dip, 13
  The Ultimate Creamed Corn, 152
Creamed corn, ultimate, 152
Creamed Potatoes with Garden Peas,
    206
Creamy Chicken and Wild Rice
    Soup, 39
Creamy Split Pea Soup, 40, *41*
Crowd-Pleasing Chili, 172
Currant-cherry sauce, ham with,
    186, 201
Curry(ied)
  cauliflower, 150, *151*
  pork stew, 58, *59*

D
Desserts, 71
  Brown Sugar Strawberries, 71
  Honey-Chocolate Sundaes, 71
  Rice and Raisin Pudding, 71
Dijon, honey-, ham, 126, *127*
Dips
  Cheesy Chicken and Peppers Dip,
    18, *19*
  Hot Artichoke and Spinach Dip,
    14, *15*
  Hot Nacho Bean Dip, 12
  Party Crab Dip, 16
  Pizza Fondue, 20, *21*
  Sausage and Pepperoni Dip, 22
  Smoky Bacon and Gruyère Dip, 13

E
Easy homemade breads, 43
Easy Savory Baked Beans, 136
Eggplant, in Greek-Style Veggies, 153
Enchilada sauce, in Cheesy Chicken
    and Peppers Dip, 18, *19*

F
Fettuccini, in Holiday Chicken
    Alfredo, 188, *189*

Finishing touches, 107
Fisherman's Wharf Seafood Stew,
    52, *53*
Flatbread, triple-cheese, 43
Fondue, pizza, 20, *21*
Food-safety check, 8–9
French-fried onions, in
  Beef and Creamy Potato Casserole,
    116
  Sour Cream and Onion Potato
    Casserole, 154
French onion biscuits, quick, 43
French Onion Meatballs, 28, *29*
French onion soup, in Hamburger
    Hash, 173
Frittata, supper ham, 128
Fruit. *See also specific types*
  chutney, ham with, 87
  salad, honey-lime, 71

G
Garbanzo beans. *See* Beans
Garlic
  Garlic Chicken with Italian Beans,
    98, *99*
  Garlic-Parmesan Smashed
    Potatoes, *125*, 204, *205*
  Rosemary-Garlic Beef Roast, 198
Get-togethers, 17
Glossary of cooking terms, 213
Greek-Style Veggies, 153
Green chile. *See* Chile, green
Gruyère, smoky bacon and, dip, 13
Gumbo, bayou, *36*, 46

H
Ham
  Brazilian Saffron Chicken and
    Rice, 96, *97*
  Ham and Asparagus Chowder, 129
  Ham and Lentil Stew, 90, *91*
  Ham with Cheesy Potatoes, 88, *89*
  Ham with Currant-Cherry Sauce,
    186, 201
  Ham with Fruit Chutney, 87
  Honey-Dijon Ham, 126, *127*
  Southern-Style String Beans, 146,
    147
  Supper Ham Frittata, 128

Hamburger Hash, 173
Harvest Sausage-Vegetable Casserole, 75
Hash, hamburger, 173
Hassle-Free Holidays, 186–211
Helpful nutrition and cooking information, 212–13
Herbed Potatoes and Peppers, 156, *157*
High altitude tips, 9
Hoisin ribs, Asian, 82, *83*
Holiday Chicken Alfredo, 188, *189*
Holiday Meals Made Easy, 192–93
    menus, 193
Hominy, chunky chicken chili with, 62
Honey-Chocolate Sundaes, 71
Honey-Cranberry Butternut Squash, 210
Honey-Dijon Ham, 126, *127*
Honey-Lime Fruit Salad, 71
Horseradish Sauce, 108
Horseradish sour cream, corned beef brisket with, 79
Hot and Spicy Riblets, 31
Hot Artichoke and Spinach Dip, 14, *15*
Hot Dog and Bacon Roll-Ups, 25
Hot Nacho Bean Dip, 12
Hunter's-Style Pork Roast, 117

I

Intermittent cookers, 6
Italian beef tips, zesty, 80
Italian Meatballs with Marinara Sauce, 114, *115*

J

Jambalaya, chicken and sausage, 174, *175*

K

Kidney beans. *See* Beans

L

Lamb stew, Scottish, 56, *57*
Leftovers, great ideas for
    Beef Roast with Shiitake Mushroom Sauce
        Beef and Asparagus Over Noodles, 104
        Chinese Beef and Broccoli, 105

Honey-Dijon Ham
    Ham and Asparagus Chowder, 129
    Supper Ham Frittata, 128
Mexican Pork Roast with Chili Sauce
    Cheesy Pork Quesadillas, 120
    Spicy Pork and Pineapple Salad, 121
Lentils
    ham and, stew, 90, *91*
    and veggies, 144
Lettuce, in
    Chicken and Bean Tacos, 162
    Make-Your-Own Taco Salad, 176
Lime, honey-, fruit salad, 71

M

Main dishes, 66–129
    meaty, 92–129
Make It and Take It, 158–185
Make-Your-Own Taco Salad, 176
Maple- and Apricot-Sauced Turkey Breast, 191
Maple baked beans, sweet, *130*, 132
Maple-Mustard Barbecued Meatballs and Sausages, 30
Maple syrup, in Maple- and Apricot-Sauced Turkey Breast, 191
Marshmallows, in Candied Sweet Potatoes, *127*, 155
Meatball(s)
    Asian, 178, *179*
    French onion, 28, *29*
    Italian, with marinara sauce, 114, *115*
    and sausages, maple-mustard barbecued, 30
    stone soup, 44, *45*
    Swedish, 180
Menus, holiday, 193
Metric conversion guide, 214
Mexican Beef Chili, 63
Mexican Beef Stew, 54, *55*
Mexican cheese blend
    in Beef and Green Chile Tortilla Dinner, 177
    in Hot Nacho Bean Dip, 12
Mexican Pork Roast with Chili Sauce, 118, *119*
Minestrone, two-bean, 42
Mini Cheeseburger Bites, 26, *27*

Molasses, in Easy Savory Baked Beans, 136
Mozzarella cheese. *See* Cheese
Mushroom(s)
    in Apple-Walnut Stuffing, 202
    in Chicken Stew, *66*, 68
    in Greek-Style Veggies, 153
    in Holiday Chicken Alfredo, 188, *189*
    in Hunter's-Style Pork Roast, 117
    in Provençal Beef with Zinfandel, 196, *197*
    Sherry Buttered Mushrooms, 145
    shiitake, sauce, beef roast with, 102, *103*
    in Spinach- and Mushroom-Stuffed Pork Roast, 199
Mushroom cream sauce, chicken breasts with, 190
Mushroom soup, in
    Beef and Creamy Potato Casserole, 116
    Beef Pot Roast with Vegetables, 78
    Chicken–Wild Rice Casserole with Dried Cherries, 69
    Ham and Asparagus Chowder, 129
    Hamburger Hash, 173
    Smoky Cheese and Potato Bake, 207
    Sour Cream and Onion Potato Casserole, 154
    Swedish Meatballs, 180
Mustard, asparagus with, 71

N

Nacho bean dip, hot, 12
New Orleans–Style Red Beans, 139
Noodles, beef and asparagus over, 104
Nutrition guidelines, 212
Nuts, in
    Chex Party Mix, 34
    Honey-Cranberry Butternut Squash, 210
    Spiced Party Nut Mix, *10*, 35

O

Okra, in Bayou Gumbo, *36*, 46
Olives, in
    Brazilian Saffron Chicken and Rice, 96, *97*

Olives, in *(cont.)*
    Greek-Style Veggies, 153
    Pizza Fondue, 20, *21*
    Zesty Italian Beef Tips, 80
Orange-Glazed Beets, 148
Orange-Pecan Butter, 208, *209*
Orange pork roast, spiced, 200

P

Parmesan cheese. *See* Cheese
Parsnips, in Southwest Vegetable
    Stew, 211
Party Crab Dip, 16
Party mix
    Chex, 34
    spiced nut, *10*, 35
Pasta dishes
    Beef and Asparagus Over Noodles,
      104
    Cheesy Ravioli Casserole, 184, *185*
    Holiday Chicken Alfredo, 188, *189*
    Slow-Simmered Spaghetti Meat
      Sauce, 113
    Two-Bean Minestrone, 42
    Zesty Italian Beef Tips, 80
Peach and Plum Salad, 71
Peanut butter, in Spicy Chicken in
    Peanut Sauce, 100
Peanuts. *See* Nuts
Pear-Apple Sauce with Cherries, 203
Peas
    black-eyed, in Black-Eyed Pea and
      Sausage Soup, 48
    black-eyed, in Southwestern Calico
      Baked Beans, 182
    green, Barley Casserole with Peas
      and Peppers, 140, *141*
    green, in Creamed Potatoes with
      Garden Peas, 206
    green, in Scottish Lamb Stew, 56, *57*
    split, in Creamy Split Pea Soup,
      40, *41*
Pecans. *See also* Nuts
    orange-, butter, 208, *209*
Pepper, bell
    Barbecued Beef and Pork
      Sandwiches, 163
    Barley Casserole with Peas and
      Peppers, 140, *141*

Barley-Vegetable Soup, 38
Beef au Jus Sandwiches, 166, *167*
Brazilian Saffron Chicken and
    Rice, 96, *97*
Caribbean Black Beans, 138
Cheesy Chicken and Peppers Dip,
    18, *19*
Chicken and Sausage Jambalaya,
    174, *175*
Chicken Breasts with Mushroom
    Cream Sauce, 190
Country French White Beans,
    134, *135*
Easy Savory Baked Beans, 136
Greek-Style Veggies, 153
Herbed Potatoes and Peppers,
    156, *157*
Holiday Chicken Alfredo, 188, *189*
Mexican Pork Roast with Chili
    Sauce, 118, *119*
Pizza Joe Sandwiches, 170
Smoky Cheese and Potato Bake,
    207
Southwest Vegetable Stew, 211
Spanish Rice with Tomatoes and
    Peppers, 142, *143*
Sweet-and-Sour Chicken, 94, *95*
Turkey Chili, *158*, 171
Pepperoni
    in Pizza Joe Sandwiches, 170
    turkey, in Pizza Fondue, 20, *21*
    in Sausage and Pepperoni Dip, 22
Pesto Vegetables, 71
Pimientos, in Caribbean Black Beans,
    138
Pineapple
    in Pineapple Carrots, 149
    preserves, in Teriyaki Smoked
      Riblets, 32, *33*
    in Spicy Pork and Pineapple Salad,
      121
    in Sweet-and-Sour Chicken,
      94, *95*
Pinto beans. *See* Beans, pinto
Pizza Fondue, 20, *21*
Pizza Joe Sandwiches, 170
Plum(s)
    peach and, salad, 71
    in Spiced Orange Pork Roast, 200

Pork recipes. *See also* Bacon; Ham
    Apricot-Glazed Pork Roast and
      Stuffing, 84, *85*
    Asian Hoisin Ribs, 82, *83*
    Barbecued Beef and Pork
      Sandwiches, 163
    Barbecued Pork Chops, 122, *123*
    Cheesy Pork Quesadillas, 120
    Chicken and Sausage Jambalaya,
      174, *175*
    Country-Style Ribs and
      Sauerkraut, 81
    Curried Pork Stew, 58, *59*
    Easy Savory Baked Beans, 136
    Green Chile and Pork Stew, 86
    Hot and Spicy Riblets, 31
    Hunter's-Style Pork Roast, 117
    Italian Meatballs with Marinara
      Sauce, 114, *115*
    Maple-Mustard Barbecued
      Meatballs and Sausages, 30
    Mexican Pork Roast with Chili
      Sauce, 118, *119*
    sausage, in Bayou Gumbo, *36*, 46
    sausage, in Sausage and Pepperoni
      Dip, 22
    sausage, in Slow-Simmered
      Spaghetti Meat Sauce, 113
    sausage, in Southwestern Calico
      Baked Beans, 182
    Savory Barbecued Ribs, 124, *125*
    Smoky Ham and Navy Bean
      Stew, 49
    Southwestern Pork Burritos,
      168, *169*
    Spiced Orange Pork Roast, 200
    Spicy Pork and Pineapple Salad,
      121
    Spinach- and Mushroom-Stuffed
      Pork Roast, 199
    Teriyaki Smoked Riblets, 32, *33*
    Tortilla Soup, 47
Potato(es)
    in Baked Potato Bar, 183
    in Barley-Vegetable Soup, 38
    beef carbonnade with, 76, *77*
    in Beef and Creamy Potato
      Casserole, 116
    in Beef Pot Roast with Vegetables, 78

cheesy, ham with, 88, *89*
in Chicken Stew, *66*, 68
in Corned Beef and Cabbage
  Dinner, 108, *109*
in Creamed Potatoes with Garden
  Peas, 206
in Creamy Split Pea Soup, 40, *41*
in Curried Pork Stew, 58, *59*
in Garlic-Parmesan Smashed
  Potatoes, *125*, 204, *205*
in Ham and Asparagus Chowder,
  129
in Hamburger Hash, 173
in Harvest Sausage-Vegetable
  Casserole, 75
in Herbed Potatoes and Peppers,
  156, *157*
in Meatball Stone Soup, 44, *45*
in Pot Roast–Style Beef Steak,
  110, *111*
in Savory Beef Short Rib Dinner,
  92, 112
in Scottish Lamb Stew, 56, *57*
in Smoky Cheese and Potato Bake,
  207
in Sour Cream and Onion Potato
  Casserole, 154
in Southwest Vegetable Stew, 211
in Supper Ham Frittata, 128
sweet, in Candied Sweet Potatoes,
  127, 155
sweet, with orange-pecan butter,
  208, *209*
in Turkey Verde, 72, *73*
in Vegetable Beef Stew, 60
Potluck Pointers, 164–65
Pot roast
  beef, with vegetables, 78
  pork, apricot-glazed, and stuffing,
    84, *85*
  Pot Roast–Style Beef Steak, 110,
    111
Pretzels
  in Chex Party Mix, 34
  in Spiced Party Nut Mix, *10*, 35
Provençal Beef with Zinfandel, 196,
  197
Pudding, rice and raisin, 71

Q

Quesadillas, cheesy pork, 120
Quick Corn Bread Sticks, 43
Quick French Onion Biscuits, 43

R

Raisin, rice and, pudding, 71
Ravioli casserole, cheesy, 184, *185*
Refried beans. See Beans, refried
Ribs, pork
  country-style, and sauerkraut, 81
  country-style, Asian hoisin, 82, *83*
  hot and spicy, 31
  savory barbecued, 124, *125*
  teriyaki smoked, 32, *33*
Rice and Raisin Pudding, 71
Rice dishes. *See also* Couscous
  Bayou Gumbo, *36*, 46
  Brazilian Saffron Chicken and Rice,
    96, *97*
  Chicken and Sausage Jambalaya,
    174, *175*
  Chinese Beef and Broccoli, 105
  Spanish Rice with Tomatoes and
    Peppers, 142, *143*
  Sweet-and-Sour Chicken, 94, *95*
  wild rice, creamy chicken and,
    soup, 39
  wild rice, in chicken–, casserole
    with dried cherries, 69
Roll-ups, hot dog and bacon, 25
Rosemary-Garlic Beef Roast, 198

S

Salads
  Black Bean and Corn Salad, 71
  Honey-Lime Fruit Salad, 71
  Make-Your-Own Taco Salad, 176
  Peach and Plum Salad, 71
  Spicy Pork and Pineapple Salad,
    121
Salsa, in
  Beef and Green Chile Tortilla
    Dinner, 177
  Cheesy Pork Quesadillas, 120
  Chicken and Bean Tacos, 162
  Green Chile and Pork Stew, 86
  Make-Your-Own Taco Salad, 176

Southwestern Calico Baked Beans,
  182
  Turkey Verde, 72, *73*
Sandwiches
  barbecued beef and pork, 163
  beef au jus, 166, *167*
  chicken, teriyaki barbecued, 160, *161*
  pizza joe, 170
Sauce
  Alfredo pasta, in Creamed Potatoes
    with Garden Peas, 206
  chile, in Mexican Pork Roast with
    Chili Sauce, 118, *119*
  currant-cherry, ham with, *186*, 201
  enchilada sauce, in Cheesy Chicken
    and Peppers Dip, 18, *19*
  horseradish, 108
  maple- and apricot-, turkey breast,
    191
  marinara, in Italian meatballs with,
    114, *115*
  marinara, in Zesty Italian Beef
    Tips, 80
  marinara, Italian meatballs with,
    114, *115*
  meat, spaghetti, slow-simmered, 113
  mushroom cream, chicken breasts
    with, 190
  peanut, spicy chicken in, 100
  pear-apple, with cherries, 203
  shiitake mushroom, beef roast with,
    102, *103*
  tomato, in Cheesy Ravioli
    Casserole, 184, *185*
  tomato, in Chicken and Bean Tacos,
    162
  tomato, in Crowd-Pleasing Chili,
    172
  tomato, in Make-Your-Own Taco
    Salad, 176
  tomato, in New Orleans–Style Red
    Beans, 139
Sauerkraut, country-style ribs and, 81
Sausage
  chicken, -vegetable casserole,
    harvest, 75
  pork, in Bayou Gumbo, *36*, 46
  pork, in Sausage and Pepperoni
    Dip, 22

Sausage *(cont.)*
  pork, in Slow-Simmered Spaghetti Meat Sauce, 113
  pork, in Southwestern Calico Baked Beans, 182
  turkey, –bean bake, 74
  turkey, -vegetable casserole, harvest, 75
Savory Barbecued Ribs, 124, *125*
Savory Beef Short Rib Dinner, *92*, 112
Scottish Lamb Stew, 56, *57*
Seafood. *See also* Shrimp
  Fisherman's Wharf Seafood Stew, 52, *53*
Sherry Buttered Mushrooms, 145
Shiitake mushroom sauce, beef roast with, 102, *103*
Shrimp
  in Bayou Gumbo, *36*, 46
  in Fisherman's Wharf Seafood Stew, 52, *53*
Simple sides and desserts, 71
Slow cooker
  converting range-top recipe to slow-cooker recipe, 8
  slow cooking mde simple, 6–9
  tips and tricks, 6–7
Slow-Simmered Spaghetti Meat Sauce, 113
Smoky Bacon and Gruyère Dip, 13
Smoky Cheese and Potato Bake, 207
Smoky Ham and Navy Bean Stew, 49
Snacks. *See* Appetizers; Dips; Party mix
Soups. *See also* Chili; Chowder; Stews
  Bayou Gumbo, *36*, 46
  Black-Eyed Pea and Sausage Soup, 48
  Creamy Chicken and Wild Rice Soup, 39
  Creamy Split Pea Soup, 40, *41*
  finishing touches for, 107
  Meatball Stone Soup, 44, *45*
  Pork Tortilla Soup, 47
  Two-Bean Minestrone, 42
Sour cream, in
  Beef and Asparagus Over Noodles, 104
  Chicken and Bean Tacos, 162

Corned Beef Brisket with Horseradish Sour Cream, 79
Ham with Cheesy Potatoes, 88, *89*
Party Crab Dip, 16
Smoky Cheese and Potato Bake, 207
Sour Cream and Onion Potato Casserole, 154
Spicy Pork and Pineapple Salad, 121
Southern-Style String Beans, 146, *147*
Southwestern Calico Baked Beans, 182
Southwestern Pinto Beans, 133
Southwestern Pork Burritos, 168, *169*
Southwest Vegetable Stew, 211
Spanish Rice with Tomatoes and Peppers, 142, *143*
Spiced Orange Pork Roast, 200
Spiced Party Nut Mix, *10*, 35
Spicy Black Bean Barbecue Chili, 64, 65
Spicy Chicken in Peanut Sauce, 100
Spicy Pork and Pineapple Salad, 121
Spinach
  artichoke and, dip, hot, 14, *15*
  in Black-Eyed Pea and Sausage Soup, 48
  in Cauliflower Curry, 150, *151*
  in Chicken and Vegetable Tortellini Stew, 50, *51*
  in Creamy Split Pea Soup, 40, *41*
  Spinach- and Mushroom-Stuffed Pork Roast, 199
Spreads. *See* Dips
Squash, butternut, honey-cranberry, 210
Stews
  Chicken and Vegetable Tortellini Stew, 50, *51*
  Chicken Stew, *66*, 68
  Curried Pork Stew, 58, *59*
  finishing touches for, 107
  Fisherman's Wharf Seafood Stew, 52, *53*
  Ham and Lentil Stew, 90, *91*
  Mexican Beef Stew, 54, *55*
  Provençal Beef with Zinfandel, 196, *197*
  Scottish Lamb Stew, 56, *57*
  Smoky Ham and Navy Bean Stew, 49

Southwest Vegetable Stew, 211
Vegetable Beef Stew, 60
Strawberries, brown sugar, 71
String beans, southern-style, 146, *147*
Stuffing
  apple-walnut, 202
  apricot-glazed pork roast and, 84, *85*
  sherried, turkey breast with, 70
Sugar, brown, strawberries, 71
Sundaes, honey-chocolate, 71
Supper Ham Frittata, 128
Swedish Meatballs, 180
Sweet-and-Sour Chicken, 94, *95*
Sweet Maple Baked Beans, *130*, 132
Sweet potatoes
  candied, *127*, 155
  with orange-pecan butter, 208, *209*

T
Table toppers for holiday table, 193
Taco(s)
  chicken and bean, 162
  white chili mini, 24
Taco seasoning mix, in
  Beef and Green Chile Tortilla Dinner, 177
  Chicken and Bean Tacos, 162
  Hot Nacho Bean Dip, 12
  Make-Your-Own Taco Salad, 176
  Mexican Beef Stew, 54, *55*
  Southwestern Calico Baked Beans, 182
  Spiced Party Nut Mix, *10*, 35
  White Chili Mini Tacos, 24
Tasty Take-Alongs for Potlucks, 165
Teriyaki
  Teriyaki Barbecued Chicken Sandwiches, 160, *161*
  Teriyaki Smoked Riblets, 32, *33*
  Turkey Teriyaki, 101
Texas-Style Barbecued Beans, 181
Tomato(es)
  chopped, in Cauliflower Curry, 150, *151*
  chopped, in Make-Your-Own Taco Salad, 176
  crushed, in Mexican Beef Stew, 54, *55*

crushed, in Slow-Simmered Spaghetti Meat Sauce, 113
crushed, Spicy Chicken in Peanut Sauce, 100
diced, in Barley-Vegetable Soup, 38
diced, in Bayou Gumbo, *36*, 46
diced, in Chicken and Sausage Jambalaya, 174, *175*
diced, in Chunky Chicken Chili with Hominy, 62
diced, in Crowd-Pleasing Chili, 172
diced, in Garlic Chicken with Italian Beans, 98, *99*
diced, in Harvest Sausage-Vegetable Casserole, 75
diced, in Herbed Potatoes and Peppers, 156, *157*
diced, in Hunter's-Style Pork Roast, 117
diced, in Lentils and Veggies, 144
diced, in Meatball Stone Soup, 44, *45*
diced, in Mexican Beef Chili, 63
diced, in Pork Tortilla Soup, 47
diced, in Provençal Beef with Zinfandel, 196, *197*
diced, in Southwestern Pork Burritos, 168, *169*
diced, in Spanish Rice with Tomatoes and Peppers, 142, *143*
diced, in Spicy Black Bean Barbecue Chili, 64, 65
diced, in Turkey Chili, *158*, 171
diced, in Two-Bean Minestrone, 42
diced, Spicy Chicken in Peanut Sauce, 100
plum, in Fisherman's Wharf Seafood Stew, 52, *53*
stewed, Southwest Vegetable Stew, 211
sun-dried, in Zesty Italian Beef Tips, 80
whole, in Curried Pork Stew, 58, *59*
Tomato paste, in
  Barbecued Beef and Pork Sandwiches, 163
  Cheesy Ravioli Casserole, 184, *185*
  Southwestern Pinto Beans, 133

Southwestern Pork Burritos, 168, *169*
Southwest Vegetable Stew, 211
Tomato sauce. See Sauce, tomato
Tortellini stew, chicken and vegetable, 50, *51*
Tortillas
  in Cheesy Pork Quesadillas, 120
  chips, in Beef and Green Chile Tortilla Dinner, 177
  in Southwestern Pork Burritos, 168, *169*
  soup, pork, 47
  in Turkey Verde, 72, *73*
Triple-Cheese Flatbread, 43
Turkey recipes
  Bacon- and Corn Bread–Stuffed Turkey Breast, 194, *195*
  Black-Eyed Pea and Sausage Soup, 48
  Harvest Sausage-Vegetable Casserole, 75
  Maple- and Apricot-Sauced Turkey Breast, 191
  Turkey Breast with Sherried Stuffing, 70
  Turkey Chili, *158*, 171
  turkey pepperoni, in Pizza Fondue, 20, *21*
  Turkey Sausage–Bean Bake, 74
  Turkey Teriyaki, 101
  Turkey Verde, 72, *73*
Two-Bean Minestrone, 42

U

Ultimate Creamed Corn, The, 152

V

Vegetable(s). *See also* Beans; Salads; *specific types*
  beef pot roast with, 78
  Caesar Vegetable Medley, 71
  chicken and, tortellini stew, 50, *51*
  Greek-style, 153
  lentils and, 144
  pesto, 71
  stew, beef, 60
  stew, southwest, 211
Vegetable juice, in Two-Bean Minestrone, 42

W

Walnuts. *See also* Nuts
  apple-, stuffing, 202
Water chestnuts, in Asian Meatballs, 178, *179*
What a great idea...leftovers
  Beef Roast with Shiitake Mushroom Sauce
    Beef and Asparagus Over Noodles, 104
    Chinese Beef and Broccoli, 105
  Honey-Dijon Ham
    Ham and Asparagus Chowder, 129
    Supper Ham Frittata, 128
  Mexican Pork Roast with Chili Sauce
    Cheesy Pork Quesadillas, 120
    Spicy Pork and Pineapple Salad, 121
Wheat berries, in Black-Eyed Pea and Sausage Soup, 48
White Chili Mini Tacos, 24
White Chili with Chicken, 61

Z

Zesty Italian Beef Tips, 80
Zinfandel wine, Provençal beef with, 196, *197*
Zucchini, in
  Greek-Style Veggies, 153
  Supper Ham Frittata, 128

Complete your cookbook library
with these *Betty Crocker* titles

Betty Crocker's Best Bread Machine Cookbook

Betty Crocker's Best Chicken Cookbook

Betty Crocker's Best Christmas Cookbook

Betty Crocker's Best of Baking

Betty Crocker's Best of Healthy and Hearty Cooking

Betty Crocker's Best-Loved Recipes

Betty Crocker's Bisquick® Cookbook

Betty Crocker's Bread Machine Cookbook

Betty Crocker's Cook It Quick

Betty Crocker's Cookbook, 9th Edition - *The* **BIG RED** *Cookbook*®

Betty Crocker's Cookbook, Bridal Edition

Betty Crocker's Cookie Book

Betty Crocker's Cooking for Two

Betty Crocker's Cooky Book, Facsimile Edition

Betty Crocker's Cooking Basics

Betty Crocker's Diabetes Cookbook

Betty Crocker's Easy Slow Cooker Dinners

Betty Crocker's Eat and Lose Weight

Betty Crocker's Entertaining Basics

Betty Crocker's Flavors of Home

Betty Crocker's Great Grilling

Betty Crocker's Healthy New Choices

Betty Crocker's Indian Home Cooking

Betty Crocker's Italian Cooking

Betty Crocker's Kids Cook!

Betty Crocker's Kitchen Library

Betty Crocker's Living with Cancer Cookbook

Betty Crocker's Low-Fat Low-Cholesterol Cooking Today

Betty Crocker's New Cake Decorating

Betty Crocker's New Chinese Cookbook

Betty Crocker's A Passion for Pasta

Betty Crocker's Picture Cook Book, Facsimile Edition

Betty Crocker's Quick & Easy Cookbook

Betty Crocker's Slow Cooker Cookbook

Betty Crocker's Ultimate Cake Mix Cookbook

Betty Crocker's Vegetarian Cooking